Teaching WITH Care

Cultivating Personal Qualities That Make a Difference

LENORE SANDEL

Editor

INTERNATIONAL
Reading Association
800 BARKSDALE ROAD, PO BOX 8139
NEWARK, DE 19714-8139, USA
www.reading.org

The International Reading Association attempts, through its publications, to provide a forum for a wide spectrum of opinions on reading. This policy permits divergent viewpoints without implying the endorsement of the Association.

Director of Publications Dan Mangan
Editorial Director, Books and Special Projects Teresa Curto
Managing Editor, Books Shannon T. Fortner
Acquisitions and Developmental Editor Corinne M. Mooney
Associate Editor Charlene M. Nichols
Associate Editor Elizabeth C. Hunt
Production Editor Amy Messick
Books and Inventory Assistant Rebecca A. Fetterolf
Permissions Editor Janet S. Parrack
Assistant Permissions Editor Tyanna L. Collins
Production Department Manager Iona Muscella
Supervisor, Electronic Publishing Anette Schütz
Senior Electronic Publishing Specialist R. Lynn Harrison
Electronic Publishing Specialist Lisa M. Kochel
Proofreader Stacey Lynn Sharp

Project Editor Elizabeth C. Hunt

Cover Design, Linda Steere; Illustration, © Clipart.com

Web addresses in this book were correct as of the publication date but may have become inactive or otherwise modified since that time. If you notice a deactivated or changed Web address, please e-mail books@reading.org with the words "Website Update" in the subject line. In your message, specify the Web link, the book title, and the page number on which the link appears.

Library of Congress Cataloging-in-Publication Data

Sandel, Lenore, 1922-
  Teaching with care : cultivating personal qualities that make a difference / Lenore Sandel.
       p. cm.
  Includes bibliographical references.
  ISBN-13: 978-0-87207-558-0
  1. Effective teaching. 2. Teacher effectiveness. I. Title.
  LB1025.3.S259 2006
  371.102--dc22
                                                              2006010080

For two who fill primary roles to enable and
to ennoble, from thought to print—
my husband, Leonard, and our daughter, Susan.

Contents

SECTION II
Meeting Your Students

SECTION III

The Heart of Teaching and Learning

SECTION IV
At Day's End

Foreword

When Lenore Sandel first proposed a book of thoughts by well-known educators, she already held dozens of examples. Those early statements, mostly short and pithy, might easily have fit the mold of a daily inspiration book, but for the most part they lacked the power to sustain a teacher's will and to give the substance needed to propel a long-term vision. So Dr. Sandel expanded her quest and here gives us the variety of thoughtful statements that can prompt us to examine our beliefs and our teaching practices.

Instead of a quick thought for the day, these statements could become weekly meditations on how to lift our sights and to improve our sense of instructional direction. I certainly encourage teachers to use these short essays as part of their weekly reflection, thus giving themselves the time they need to evaluate ideas and to apply those that make sense for the direction of their instruction.

I can imagine a huge surge of benefits to children if teachers contemplated one of these essays each week for one school year. I think, too, that by doing so teachers will boost their own spirits and embrace their calling with renewed energy because a recurring theme in this book is the need for

Teaching With Care: Cultivating Personal Qualities That Make a Difference by Lenore Sandel, Editor. Copyright © 2006 by the International Reading Association.

teachers to see their personal strengths and skills as important contributions to their teaching.

Thank you, Dr. Sandel, for your persistence, which now gives us this strong and useful book.

—*Carl B. Smith, Director*
Clearinghouse for Reading, English,
and Communication
Indiana University, Bloomington

Preface

There is a unique realm in the professional life of a teacher that is shared in myriad ways: personal quality, an elusive element rarely learned through text, more often through experience or practice. To cultivate personal qualities, this collection of essays speaks to each teacher through the collaborative voices of expert educators. The book provides guideposts along the way, from text to practice, from anticipated goal to vivid reality. This book is, therefore, a reaffirmation for the experienced, an inspiration for the beginner, and a reflective renewal for all.

Although the No Child Left Behind Act of 2001 (2002) focuses especially on standards and expectations, the key factor in student learning is the teacher. *Teaching With Care: Cultivating Personal Qualities That Make a Difference* serves as a complement to texts of principles and practices of education. The essays present not an answer but a question: What do these qualities, from individual voices in education, say to a beginning teacher—or any teacher?

The contributors to this work are respected educators. They share a need to strengthen the abilities of beginning teachers through personal channels that bolster the academic knowledge base. Each contributor chose his or her own term as a

Teaching With Care: Cultivating Personal Qualities That Make a Difference by Lenore Sandel, Editor. Copyright © 2006 by the International Reading Association.

stimulus for thoughts on teaching. Their goals are to reach teachers on a personal level, approach them as individuals, and give them a sense of self in the practice of teaching within a prescribed program.

Within this volume, essays are organized into four sections to guide you through the roles and stages of becoming an excellent teacher. Section I: Getting Started describes the mindset great teachers need when beginning, but also throughout, their careers. Section II: Meeting Your Students focuses on how to interact with students on a personal, individual level. Section III: The Heart of Teaching and Learning explores ways great teachers use their personal qualities to create excellent instruction every day in the classroom. In Section IV: At Day's End, you will find final thoughts on cultivating the joy, courage, and self-knowledge you need to continue your journey as a teacher and assist others in theirs. Questions for Reflection appear at the beginning of each section to help you see the distinct voices of the contributors in a collaborative sense and to allow you to reflect on your own practice. The voices and reflections in this volume remind us as teachers, with a fervent force of professional conviction, that we are not alone and that through sharing our unique experiences, we can best enrich young lives in mind and heart.

> "Each contributor chose his or her own term as a stimulus for thoughts on teaching. Their goals are to reach teachers on a personal level, approach them as individuals, and give them a sense of self in the practice of teaching within a prescribed program."

Acknowledgments

For her expertise and generous attentions, I express my affectionate appreciation to Linda Merklin, manager of editorial services at Hofstra University, who filled many roles in the process from notes to professional text. I also express sincere gratitude to the professional staff (Elizabeth Hunt, Associate Editor; Amy Messick, Production Editor) of the International Reading Association for the astute and kindly guidance in the process of editing content and design from submission to publication of this manuscript.

—Lenore Sandel

REFERENCE

No Child Left Behind Act of 2001, Pub. L. No. 107-110, 115 Stat. 1425 (2002).

RECOMMENDED READING

Chopra, D. (2004). *Fire in the heart*. New York: Simon & Schuster

Darling-Hammond, L. (1997). *Doing what matters most: Investing in quality teaching*. Kutztown, PA: National Commission on Teaching and America's Future. (ERIC Document Reproduction Service No. ED415183)

Eisner, E. (2002). *The arts and the creation of mind*. New Haven, CT: Yale University Press.

Gardner, H. (1983). *Frames of mind: The theory of multiple intelligences*. New York: Basic Books.

Greene, M. (2001). *Releasing the imagination. Essays on education, the arts, and social change*. San Francisco: Jossey-Bass.

Palmer, P.J. (1993). *To know as we are known: Education as a spiritual journey*. San Francisco: HarperSanFrancisco.

Palmer, P.J. (1997). *The courage to teach. Exploring the inner landscape of a teacher's life*. San Francisco: Jossey-Bass.

Rogers, C. (1987). Questions I would ask myself if I were a teacher. *The Educational Forum, 51*(2), 115–122.

Wilson, S.M., & Floden, R.E. (2003). *Creating effective teachers*. New York: AACTE Publications.

About the Editor

Lenore Sandel is professor emerita in the Department of Literacy Studies (formerly Department of Reading) in the School of Education and Allied Human Services at Hofstra University, Hempstead, New York. Lenore received her Bachelor of Arts degree at Hunter College of the City University of New York and a Master of Science in reading at Hofstra University. She was the recipient of the first doctorate degree in reading awarded at Hofstra University.

Lenore's love affair with education began with student teaching, more than 60 years ago. She then served as teacher director of a U.S. government nursery school in Fort Bragg, North Carolina, established for children of World War II families. Next, with a return to civilian life, she established and directed her own nursery school. Many years as a substitute teacher led to the span of four decades at Hofstra University.

Lenore is the author of *Personal Qualities of a Language Arts Teacher* (ERIC Clearinghouse on Reading, English, and Communication & The Family Learning Association, 2002) and *Historical Development of Language—A Monograph* (ERIC Clearinghouse on Reading, English, and Communication & The Family Learning Association, 2002). Her articles have been published in *The Reading Teacher*, *Journal of Reading*, *Childhood Education*, *The Record*, *Early Years*, *Dragon Lode*, *The Horn Book*, *The English Journal*, and several ERIC guides.

Lenore and her husband, Leonard, live in Rockville Centre, Long Island, New York, where they continue as active members of the community. Their daughter, Susan, is a dance/movement therapist and published author living in Connecticut. The focus on the personal qualities of the teacher has been Lenore's philosophy throughout her career.

Contributors

Harvey Alpert
Professor Emeritus of Education
Hofstra University
Hempstead, New York, USA

Keith C. Barton
Professor of Teacher Education
University of Cincinnati
Cincinnati, Ohio, USA

Beth Berghoff
Associate Professor of Language Education
Indiana University—Purdue University Indianapolis
Indianapolis, Indiana, USA

Nancy Parks Bertrand
Professor of Elementary and Special Education
Middle Tennessee State University
Murfreesboro, Tennessee, USA

Rhonda Clements
Professor of Education
Manhattanville College
Purchase, New York, USA

Lyn Corno
Adjunct Professor of Education and Psychology
Teachers College
Columbia University
New York, New York, USA

Bernice E. Cullinan
Professor Emerita of Education
New York University
New York, New York, USA

Lynne T. Díaz-Rico
Professor of Education
California State University, San Bernardino
San Bernardino, California, USA

Kieran Egan
Professor of Education
Simon Fraser University
Burnaby, British Columbia, Canada

Ruth D. Farrar
Professor of Literacy Education
    and Coordinator of Graduate Programs in Reading
Bridgewater State College
Bridgewater, Massachusetts, USA

Yetta M. Goodman
Regents Professor Emerita
University of Arizona
Tucson, Arizona, USA

Jerome C. Harste
Distinguished Professor Emeritus of Language
    Education
Indiana University
Bloomington, Indiana, USA

Thomas R. Hoerr
Head of School
New City School
St. Louis, Missouri, USA

Wayne B. Jennings
Executive Director
International Association for Learning Alternatives
St. Paul, Minnesota, USA

Ellen H. Katz
President
Mentor Talk, Inc.
New York, New York, USA

Lilian G. Katz
Codirector
Clearinghouse of Early Education and Parenting
University of Illinois
Champaign, Illinois, USA

Mary M. Kitagawa
Fifth- and Sixth-Grade Teacher (Retired)
Mark's Meadow School
Amherst, Massachusetts, USA

Karen M. Landsman
Teacher of Prekindergarten and Kindergarten
Temple Israel of Lawrence
Lawrence, New York, USA

David E. Ludlam
Associate Professor Emeritus of Education
State University of New York at Fredonia
Fredonia, New York, USA

J. Dan Marshall
Professor of Education
Pennsylvania State University
University Park, Pennsylvania, USA

Hugh Thomas McCracken
Professor Emeritus of English Education
Youngstown State University
Youngstown, Ohio, USA

John R. McIntyre
Professor of Education and Coordinator
    of the Graduate Program in Educational
    Administration and Supervision
Caldwell College
Caldwell, New Jersey, USA

Terry L. Murphy
Professor of English Education
University of Maine at Fort Kent
Fort Kent, Maine, USA

Karen F. Osterman
Professor of Educational Leadership
Hofstra University
Hempstead, New York, USA

Patricia O. Richards
Professor of Education and Reading
Salisbury University
Salisbury, Maryland, USA

Susan A. Schiller
Professor of English
Central Michigan University
Mt. Pleasant, Michigan, USA

Gregory A. Smith
Professor of Education
Lewis & Clark College Graduate School of Education
    and Counseling
Portland, Oregon, USA

Lynda Stone
Professor of Philosophy of Education
University of North Carolina at Chapel Hill
Chapel Hill, North Carolina, USA

Judith A. Sykes
Author
Brain-Friendly School Libraries
Westport, Connecticut, USA

Michael P. Wolfe
Executive Director
Kappa Delta Pi
Indianapolis, Indiana, USA

SECTION I

Getting Started

QUESTIONS FOR REFLECTION

1. Consider Keith C. Barton's ideas on vision. What do you see as your own personal vision? Has it changed, and, if so, in what ways, since you decided to become a teacher?

2. How does your passion for teaching (Terry L. Murphy) help you steer the course of your vision? How do you plan to balance the energy needed to teach and follow a curriculum (Ellen H. Katz) with your personal passions?

3. Theory (Jerome C. Harste) extends beyond rigid methods and procedures. How would your personal theory on teaching grow by cultivating curiosity (Patricia O. Richards) and wonder (Karen M. Landsman)?

Vision

KEITH C. BARTON

"You have to see past that test, you have to believe that you're preparing [students] for the next grade level, for the next level of schooling, and for their lifetimes. You have to think of it that way, in the bigger picture. That's what drives my instruction to be more challenging and to be more integrated, because the real world is challenging, the real world is integrated."

—Leslie King (Barton, 2005, p. 28)

Most teachers enter the profession because they have a vision: They want to accomplish something in the lives of young people. Some want to help students think critically about social issues; others want to nurture students' creative potential. Some teachers want students to develop pride, confidence, and self-esteem. Some want them to feel safe and cared for. Still others hope to nurture students' love of history, or chemistry, or reading. All these are admirable and praiseworthy visions, and all can have an important impact on the lives of students. Differences among teachers lie not so much in the precise *content* of their visions but in how well they use those visions to guide their daily decisions. Teachers who keep their visions foremost in mind will have meaningful and rewarding careers, while those whose visions are overwhelmed by the demands of the job will become frustrated and ineffective.

> "Differences among teachers lie not so much in the precise *content* of their visions but in how well they use those visions to guide their daily decisions."

Everyone knows someone who does not drive well—someone who clutches the steering wheel tightly, watches the road intently, and jerks the car from side to side every few seconds. Such ineffective drivers use low-aim steering— that is, they watch the section of the highway directly in front of them and make constant adjustments to keep the car between the lines. The result is an unpleasant, jerky ride. Good drivers, on the other hand, use high-aim steering. They keep their sights focused on a point farther down the road, and they steer toward that destination. Their adjustments are effortless and almost unconscious, and their passengers enjoy a smooth and pleasant ride.

The distinction between low-aim and high-aim steering applies equally well to the classroom. Every day as a teacher, you face countless distractions—the child whose nose is bleeding, paperwork that must be completed immediately, the computer that does not work, the mislaid T-shirt order forms. Some teachers spend their days fixated on these distractions, pulling their students (and colleagues) along with them in a bumpy ride of continual reaction and adjustment. However, focusing on each new crisis is a sure path to disappointment, because the distractions never end. At the end of the day, the nosebleed may have been stopped and the order forms recovered, but the teacher can reflect on few accomplishments of any real significance.

In contrast, some teachers use the equivalent of high-aim steering in their professional lives. They focus attention on their ultimate goal—their vision—rather than the steady stream of distractions that come with the job. These teachers deal with the same complications and annoyances as everyone else, but, like good drivers, they set their sights on a point farther down the road. They keep the minor issues in perspective because they are more concerned with the vision that brought them to teaching in the first place. When their day is over, they have forgotten the malfunctioning computer and the rushed paperwork. Their thoughts are occupied with larger and longer range concerns: how well they are helping students think critically, nurturing their creativity, developing their self-esteem, or helping them feel cared for. These are the thoughts that are rewarding—the reflections that come from vision.

REFERENCE

Barton, K.C. (2005). "I'm not saying these are going to be easy": Wise practice in an urban elementary school. In E.A. Yeager & O.L. Davis, Jr. (Eds.), *Wise practice in social studies teaching: Possibilities in the age of high stakes testing* (pp. 11–31). Greenwich, CT: Information Age Publishing.

Passion

TERRY L. MURPHY

"Education is not the filling of a pail,
but the lighting of a fire."

—WILLIAM BUTLER YEATS (1865–1939)

The word *passion* brings to mind images of relationships, images of affairs, images of love, and all of the various nuisances of hot and cold connotations that may be applied to the vast spectrum of interpretations associated with the very idea of passion. And passion is an idea. It is arbitrary, an abstraction relative to contextual settings, dependent upon living organisms to give to it the various meanings that may be derived from it. Then, once related to a contextual setting, the *idea of passion* becomes something quite concrete, something quite alive.

So, if passion is alive, then all things in the natural world possess it. When we witness flowers blooming or birds migrating, we witness passion. Of course, people, too, are passionate, passionate about many things: themselves, others, their endeavors.

Teaching With Care: Cultivating Personal Qualities That Make a Difference
by Lenore Sandel, Editor. Copyright © 2006 by the International Reading Association.

We recognize these people when we see them. They are motivated, curious, dynamic, and almost always interesting. They draw our attention to them; we learn from them, and some of us may desire to be like them. Passion is this desire to be something that we are not but might be; to become something or someone else that we were not but could be; and to believe that this is within the grasp of the realm of human potential, in actuality, to metamorphose ourselves.

> "Passion is this desire to be something that we are not but might be; to become something or someone else that we were not but could be; and to believe that this is within the grasp of the realm of human potential, in actuality, to metamorphose ourselves."

Many people, for many reasons, stop believing in themselves; they lose contact with their passion. Children, though, are not this type of people, for they are directly connected to their passions. They are the most passionate people I know. Witness a playground at recess time or a schoolyard at the close of a school day and you witness collected masses of passion. Yes, children are the most passionate people I know. They are infinitely motivated, infinitely curious, infinitely dynamic, and infinitely interesting, all of them. They are constantly learning. They demand answers to their questions, seek an understanding of their world, and their one burning desire is to be just like us, those adults who surround them. If we have lost contact with our passion, what is there for them to desire?

Yes, passion is about the relationships we have with every living and nonliving thing with which and with whom we come in contact. It is about the affairs we establish within those relationships. And it is about the love we have for what we do in those relationships and affairs. Passion varies only in degree, not in kind, for there is only one kind of passion. It is the very stuff of life and of living. It is responsible for our very existence; without it, we would be zombies, people without souls, people without hope, people without humanity. Children should be allowed to pursue their passions and should be surrounded by people who are passionate. We should settle for nothing less.

Energy

ELLEN H. KATZ

"Energy and persistence alter all things."

—BENJAMIN FRANKLIN (1706–1790)

nergy is defined as the capacity for action or accomplishment and is, therefore, an essential quality for teachers. Teaching is a very demanding profession. Many people think that teaching is just a 9:00 a.m.–3:00 p.m. job. Not so. Frequently teachers work through their lunch hour or stay after school to work with students. In addition, many hours of research and planning are necessary to conduct classes—and these hours are spent after school and on weekends because it is not possible to do this work during the school day. Other responsibilities such as budgeting, taking inventory of supplies, and ordering equipment also consume time. Teachers must attend endless committee and department meetings. There are also parent–teacher meetings and open house nights for parents. I often think of how many times the copy machine broke down and the hours I spent repairing

Teaching With Care: Cultivating Personal Qualities That Make a Difference by Lenore Sandel, Editor. Copyright © 2006 by the International Reading Association.

it, plus the hours I spent on what was called my "free period" to set up a lab or class activity.

Teaching is also a year-round job, not just 10 months. During summers, teachers often sharpen their skills by attending college classes or workshops to learn new techniques. Still others take courses during the school year. Teachers are frequently found in their classrooms before school commences in September to set up

> "Teaching is a very demanding profession."

their rooms. Elementary school teachers spend hours preparing individual progress reports for students four times a year. Teachers on the secondary level often assist students with their career choices or in preparing recommendations or essays for those seeking admittance to college or applying for scholarships.

To be an excellent teacher, you must cultivate your energy not only for the rigors of everyday work but also for the personal joys of teaching and learning.

Theory

JEROME C. HARSTE

*"Not only what we teach, but how we teach,
affects what is learned."*

—Douglas Barnes (1975, p. 7)

While other people may see methods as formulaic step-by-step procedures for how things are to be taught, this is not the way I think about methods. Such thinking has given methods a bad name, which is more than unfortunate. Methods are too important to be abandoned, dismissed, or walked away from. Methods are, from my perspective, instructional practices derived from theory.

How you view learners and the learning process affects—and rightfully ought to affect—how you go about supporting learners and the learning process. The social practices you put in place, based on your beliefs, are what I see as methods. And in my view, methods make a big difference. If learning is seen as an active process, then the social practices you put in place need to allow children choice as well as

Teaching With Care: Cultivating Personal Qualities That Make a Difference by Lenore Sandel, Editor. Copyright © 2006 by the International Reading Association.

agency. If learning is a social process, then collaboration and the opportunity to learn from and with others is important. If language is a meaning-making process (very few people I know learn to read for the sheer pleasure of sounding out words or learn to write to see how many words they can spell correctly), then how you present language for purposes of instruction makes a difference. If we want children to question the authority of text and how it positions them, then what we do to support this critical perspective makes a difference. It does not make a difference every once in a while—it makes a difference all of the time. This is method as it suggests a set of social practices that characterize how you teach and how you engage students.

Teachers often complain that issues like this are "too theoretical." What they want are practical ideas that work. I would argue that nothing is more practical than theory. In fact, theory and practice go hand in hand. What every educator should aim for, in my estimation, is theoretical practice, or said differently, a sound set of beliefs upon which to base the instructional decisions that are made in the classroom.

However, the process does not always go from theory to practice. Sometimes theory is grounded, or evolving from practice, but for that to happen teachers have to reflect on social practices and generate some larger theoretical premise. That is why I associate methods and theory with some of the best teachers I know. Following Schon (1983), I call them "reflective practitioners."

Just because something works does not make it worthwhile. Worksheets work. They keep students busy, but do they teach what we want students to learn? Frank Smith (1982) says that the problem is not learning. Students are learning all of the time. The problem is that what they may be learning is not what we thought we were teaching. Children learn to hate reading, for example, by the very way we teach reading. If we want to create literate individuals who read, we need to teach reading (engage in sets of social practices in the classroom) in such a manner so that children come to value this form of literate activity and see its benefit. This is method as well as practical theory and theoretical practice.

> "If we want to create literate individuals who read, we need to teach reading (engage in sets of social practices in the classroom) in such a manner so that children come to value this form of literate activity and see its benefit."

A theory is a system of beliefs that we have developed over time and through experience. With more and more experience, our theories of the world as well as our theories of teaching become more and more fleshed out. There is a difference between acting on experience, however, and acting reflectively based on experience. The first is dangerous—we repeat something because it worked. The second is generative. We now have a bigger principle we understand that can help us modify as well as generate bigger and better social practices. You do not have to be conscious of a theory to have one, but you do have to be conscious of a theory to outgrow it.

Both teachers and children hold theories of reading, whether or not they are aware that they hold these theories. Just watch them: Their behaviors always point to the types of theories they hold. Children who see reading as a sounding-out process display reading behaviors that differ from the behaviors displayed by children who see reading as a meaning-making process. Similarly, teachers who see reading as a matter of breaking the letter–sound code teach differently than teachers who see reading as a meaning-making process. Our beliefs about reading, our beliefs about children, our beliefs about social class all interact.

REFERENCES

Barnes, D. (1975). *From communication to curriculum*. New York: Penguin.

Schon, D.A. (1983). *The reflective practitioner: How professionals think in action*. New York: Basic Books.

Smith, F. (1982). *Understanding reading* (3rd ed.). New York: Holt, Rinehart and Winston.

Curiosity

PATRICIA O. RICHARDS

"The whole art of teaching is only the art of awakening the natural curiosity of young minds for the purpose of satisfying it afterwards."

—ANATOLE FRANCE (1844–1924)

I cannot imagine choosing to teach without loving to learn, just as I cannot imagine remaining vital, personally and professionally, without a constant desire to know. Curiosity is the basis for inquiry and understanding. It means perpetual wondering about the hows and whys of our world past, present, and future; real and imagined. The more we know, the more we understand. And ironically, the more certainties we discover, the more unknowns we uncover.

Teaching is not merely dispensing information. Anatole France speaks of awakening curiosity, not of providing both the questions and the answers. While teachers rarely have the luxury of creating an inquiry-based curriculum derived solely from students' interests, we *can* create environments that foster curiosity. I see teachers do this artfully by positioning themselves as colearners, generating interest and excitement through question posing and speculation.

The most influential teachers in my life were teachers by example, rather than by profession. My grandmother had little formal education, but she has an innate curiosity that compelled her to seek out and embrace new experiences throughout her life. The word I associate most with her is "why." She has always been intrigued by the "why" of things. She is just as likely to ask that question with regard to family news as with world events.

Another influential teacher is my mother, who did not become a teacher by profession until very late in her career as a nurse. She is voraciously curious and an avid reader. Her interests are wide-ranging. Like her mother, she is also interested in the "why" of things. She is an independent, critical thinker, unafraid of taking unpopular perspectives and never timid about sharing her viewpoint. Her opinions are informed by her insightful observations and her critical analysis of information. She constantly questions everything, including her own understandings, and encouraged her children to do so, too.

Curiosity is a disposition that was modeled and fostered for me at home. I regret school was a very different situation, one that I found stifling and dreary during the first two years. My teachers rigidly imposed prescriptive curricula and materials on all of their students. The classroom was a joyless place in which the teacher raised the questions, and the students provided the expected answer. Compliance was rewarded; inquisitiveness was not valued. It was not until the third grade that I again encountered an adult who exhibited curiosity. I realize now that she, too, had curricula and materials that varied little from year to year. But she was able and willing to go beyond the givens. She stimulated our interests and encouraged wondering. She welcomed questions beyond the confines of our textbooks. She would suggest sources for finding answers, including the library and our parents, but she cleverly refrained from doling out answers. She made every third grader in her classroom feel empowered.

> "Teachers need to teach students how to find information in response to questions that can be answered, how to pose questions in order to discover answers, and how to deal productively with questions that have no answers."

As a reading teacher, one of my favorite questions after reading a selection, whether fiction or nonfiction, is "What do you wonder?" Another is "Does anything bother you?" These questions fuel curiosity by encouraging students to connect personally and critically with the author and with one another. The questions encourage multiple interpretations and divergent responses. These discussions often lead to further investigations. They also provide an authentic context for realizing that not everyone perceives things identically and that there is not always a single, right answer. In some instances, we may have to agree to disagree. Civil discourse, problem posing, and problem solving are central to teaching and learning and are essential life skills.

Curiosity is the attribute that prompts action research. As teachers, we need to seek information about the children we teach. We need to investigate instructional approaches and techniques by reading the professional literature. We need to be informed by that research and be curious enough to try new approaches. There are multiple paths in learning, and a teacher's quest is to find the best paths for students, every day in every content area, and year after year.

Curiosity is a vital characteristic in teaching because no one can ever know all there is to know. Teachers need to teach students how to find information in response to questions that can be answered, how to pose questions in order to discover answers, and how to deal productively with questions that have no answers. Ambiguity is a fact of life. In order to do all of this, teachers need to be acquainted with many disciplines and approaches to seeking and acquiring knowledge. We need to recognize the many forms curiosity takes and share those forms with our students. Those who are genuinely curious thrive in a challenging and dynamic environment.

Wonder

KAREN M. LANDSMAN

"If a child is to keep alive his inborn sense of wonder, he needs the companionship of at least one adult who can share it, rediscovering with him the joy, excitement and mystery of the world we live in."

—RACHEL CARSON (1964/1998, P. 41)

I have always loved the image conjured by the line "And what to my wondrous eyes should appear..." from Clement Clarke Moore's "A Visit From St. Nicholas" (1823), more commonly known as "'Twas the Night Before Christmas." That short phrase makes me imagine a wide-eyed, awestruck child. Likewise, a good classroom is filled with that excitement and wonder that reverberate in the souls of the children and their teachers.

My first teaching assignment was in a third-grade class. I can remember experiencing that feeling of wonder with a youngster who suddenly understood the concept of the cycle of life. We were talking about the proverbial chicken and egg and which came first when Alexandra jumped up and

Teaching With Care: Cultivating Personal Qualities That Make a Difference by Lenore Sandel, Editor. Copyright © 2006 by the International Reading Association.

exclaimed, "I get it! It just keeps going round and round—like lions, and fish, and people, too!" The joy inherent in the discovery was apparent for her and for me.

Later on, I taught 3-year-olds in a nursery school. One day the children were trying to build in the block corner but were unsuccessful and quite frustrated. They had been talking about Disneyland, so I told them, "Let's build a plane to take us there." We "flew" to Disneyland many times that day and together entered a delightful fantasy world that I have never forgotten.

Other small moments have filled me with an awesome feeling of wonder throughout the years: A small spider crosses the classroom floor and excitement and curiosity fill the room; one of the children begins to understand how to use letters to create words and read; a smile lights up the face of the shyest kindergartner in the class, and he spontaneously hugs the teacher. However, more than any regular classroom's events can inspire and touch the heart of a teacher, it is the experience of working with children whose lives are challenged physically, mentally, or emotionally that surpasses them all. I was privileged to be allowed to work with children with autism. They ranged from ages 2 to 12, and they were always interesting and a constant source of wonder. Children with autism offer the teacher an opportunity to observe, reach out, and eventually connect with an active mind that cannot express itself in the usual manner. To really know the feelings of wonder and of mystery, you should consider joining these children on their search to understand the world in a very different way. When you see the light of understanding glimmer in their eyes, you, too, will be grateful to have had the opportunity to be working with special children.

Regardless of the students you teach, if you come to a classroom eager to be part of the excitement of watching young minds blossom, you will soon discover the added bonus of enhancing your own sense of wonder. The good teacher so often becomes the student and in that capacity emerges a better teacher. Without wide-eyed curiosity and the ability to be astonished, you can never fully experience the joy of wondering and pass it on to your students. Enter this world, and every day you will be able to say, "And what to my wondrous eyes should appear...!"

> "Regardless of the students you teach, if you come to a classroom eager to be part of the excitement of watching young minds blossom, you will soon discover the added bonus of enhancing your own sense of wonder. The good teacher so often becomes the student and in that capacity emerges a better teacher."

REFERENCE

Carson, R. (1998). *The sense of wonder*. New York: HarperCollins. (Original work published 1964)

SECTION II

Meeting Your Students

1. Respect (Lilian G. Katz) is one of the key factors in any human interaction, and this extends specifically to cultural sensitivity (Lynne T. Díaz-Rico). In what ways do you currently demonstrate respect to your students? How could you improve the culture of respect in your classroom?

2. True partnership (Harvey Alpert) between students and teachers is difficult to achieve. In what ways in your classroom do you currently foster the trust needed (Mary M. Kitagawa) to facilitate this balance? Use the climate of trust and partnership you create to inspire students' self-expression (Bernice E. Cullinan) and imagination (Kieran Egan).

3. Through love (Wayne B. Jennings), many students who previously seemed unreachable may develop the confidence and motivation to succeed. Think of a particular student in your classroom whom you do not favor. How might you show empathy (Karen F. Osterman) and caring (Nancy Parks Bertrand) with that student? What changes might you see as a result?

Respect

LILIAN G. KATZ

"The secret of education is respecting the pupil."

—RALPH WALDO EMERSON (1803–1882)

One of the essential attributes of a good teacher, at every level of education, from preschool to graduate school, is the disposition to respect learners. The concept of respect is an elusive one, and very difficult to define. But it is one of those elements of human relationships that we seem to know when we see it, when it is there and when it is not.

Respecting the learner means, among other things, attributing positive qualities, intentions, and expectations, even when the available evidence casts doubts on them. A respectful relationship between the teacher and the learner is one marked by treating learners with dignity, listening closely and attentively to what your learners say, and also looking out for what they seem reluctant to say. Respect also includes treating the learner as a sensible person, even though that sometimes requires a stretch of the teacher's imagination. This element of respect implies that as teachers we should resist the tempta-

Teaching With Care: Cultivating Personal Qualities That Make a Difference by Lenore Sandel, Editor. Copyright © 2006 by the International Reading Association.

tion to talk to young children in silly, sweet voices, heaping empty praise on them, and giving them certificates indicating that a smiling bear believes they are special. This disrespectful strategy makes a mockery of teaching. After all, teaching is about helping students to make a better, deeper, and fuller sense of their experience and derive deep satisfaction from that experience. Education is not about amusement, excitement, and entertainment.

> "A respectful relationship between the teacher and the learner is one marked by treating learners with dignity, listening closely and attentively to what your learners say, and also looking out for what they seem reluctant to say."

Respectful teaching conveys through the relationship between the teacher and the learner a confidence in the child's potential ability to overcome difficulties and to persist in the face of some inevitable obstacles. A respectful teacher is one who helps children who have persisted in the face of setbacks to accept their limitations gracefully and to be satisfied and gratified that they have done their very best.

A respectful teacher is also one who helps students, even the young ones, to evaluate their own accomplishments as they progress, not in terms of whether their work is good or bad, or right or wrong, but in terms of other criteria they can gradually develop the habit of using. For example, you can ask in a serious and respectful way, "Is the drawing as complete as you want it to be?" or "Does the story you wrote (or told) include as much detail as you think it should or could?" Even preschoolers have been observed to respond to such queries thoughtfully and to indicate the beginning of a lifelong disposition to evaluate their own efforts thoughtfully.

Along similar lines, another important aspect of respectfulness in teacher–learner relationships is honesty. Teachers are often so eager to encourage children by praising them that after a while they develop the habit of issuing streams of empty and false praise that many children begin to see through and to dismiss as the inevitable, useless, and boring response of a kind and well-meaning teacher. Being honest when evaluating a student's work does not imply any kind of insulting or humiliating response to a child's efforts. Rather it implies conveying in dignified and serious tones how some piece of work might have been better or could be improved, or even redone. A teacher can often reassure a child by suggesting he or she give the story or poem or picture another try, perhaps emphasizing or explaining that others will be more able to enjoy the story or poem with the suggested revisions.

Another major element of respectfulness in professional behavior is the disposition to treat all of those we serve with dignity, even when we disagree with them, or even perhaps dislike them. To respect, accept, and treat with dignity a child we like, enjoy, and agree with is easy. We all can do that easily. But it takes a true professional to be respectful and accepting of a child you might wish were absent from the class. To be a professional also means treating with dignity and acceptance parents and other adults we might dislike or with whom we disagree.

Respect cannot be enacted or conveyed by gestures, trick phrases, or anything phony. It can only be communicated when the teacher's feelings toward learners are based on the deeply and profoundly held assumption that all humans are created equal—not equally tall, equally mathematical, equally athletic, musical, poetic, or analytical. But we are all equally human in that we all have dreams, hopes, wishes, fears, and fantasies, and we all want and deserve to be treated with dignity and respect.

Cultural Sensitivity

LYNNE T. DÍAZ-RICO

*"As a novice teacher, I was overwhelmed...my
students were economically, socially, and
emotionally needy. Unknowingly, I had taken on the
job of ESL teacher and part-time social worker....
Unfortunately, I was unable to help them as much as
I should have because I didn't recognize or
understand the hidden values and expectations of
the school community. How could I explain to the
mainstream students and staff what I didn't even
consciously know myself?"*

—JUDIE HAYNES (2004, PP. 8–9)

Knowledge about the culture of the students is
an essential part of teaching. When students
and teacher share a culture, students see the
teacher's values, beliefs, and behaviors as an ex-
tension of those of their parents, and the expectations of the teacher and the parents strike a
consonant chord. However, in situations in which
the teacher and students were not socialized into

the same culture, intercultural misunderstandings or even conflict can occur.

Throughout the United States, 47 million people (almost one fifth of the population) speak a language other than English at home (United States Census Bureau, 2004). Of this population, some parents whose children attend U.S. schools are deeply committed to assimilating into mainstream American values. Other parents are resistant to change and, rather than acclimating to the culture of the school, they expect teachers to respect their diversity. By understanding the world of your students, you can meet parents more than halfway as they learn the cultural norms of school life. Understanding the ways that culture influences attitudes and behavior will help you to become an intercultural educator, with an expanded repertoire of strategies to meet the needs of diverse students.

As an intercultural educator, you will need to cultivate three main skills and responsibilities: an understanding of cultural diversity, an engagement in the struggle for equity, and a commitment to promoting educational achievement for all students. With this preparation, you can use intercultural communication effectively in the classroom.

First, understanding cultural diversity means being able to recognize the role of culture and language in learning, explore your own culture, and compare how diverse primary cultures socialize individuals differently. When teachers understand their own culturally derived values, attitudes, and behaviors, they can, in turn, map the differences between students' cultures and their own, and use culturally responsive teaching behaviors. Those who are willing to engage in self-assessment activities can achieve rich insights. Likewise, ongoing discussion between individuals of different cultures provides opportunity for self-knowledge and personal growth.

Second, to engage in the struggle for equity, teachers must work within their schools and classrooms for equal opportunity for nonmainstream students, using vigilance to detect customs and policies that unfairly privilege some students at the expense of others. They must also work to combat prejudice in themselves and others. Many U.S. teachers, however well intentioned, enter teacher education with racial, ethnic, and class prejudices. The best way to assess your own fairness is to ask a bicultural person to observe classroom interaction and offer feedback, monitoring the students' oral participation.

> "When teachers understand their own culturally derived values, attitudes, and behaviors, they can, in turn, map the differences between students' cultures and their own, and use culturally responsive teaching behaviors."

Third, promoting educational achievement means working with the culturally influenced learning styles of each student, or the ways by which individuals in a specific culture are taught to acquire and retain knowledge and solve problems. For example, the compliant attentiveness of some students from Asian cultures can be limiting when the class is brainstorming ideas. Teachers should take the lead in encouraging values and behaviors that enhance achievement, while working with parents and community members to modify a student's attitudes that may limit school success.

In addition, you can understand more about your students' cultures by realizing that any learning that takes place is built on previous learning. Students have learned the basic patterns of living and learning in the context of their families. All cultures provide an adequate pattern of living for their members. Therefore, no children are culturally deprived. Certain communities may exist in relative poverty; that is, they are not equipped with middle class resources. Poverty, however, should not be equated with cultural deprivation. Every community's culture incorporates vast knowledge about successful living—social customs, the use of space and time, how to work and play, what occupations to aspire toward, and how to use education to further career goals. Teachers can utilize this cultural knowledge to organize students' learning. The students' cultures can also be a rich source of learning activities that enrich the standard curriculum.

Perceiving and valuing cultural diversity goes a long way toward understanding individual differences. In a multicultural classroom, there may be no single best way for you to teach or for students to learn. The key for the intercultural educator rests within: to foster the personal qualities of sensitivity, flexibility, and openness to new ideas and insights.

REFERENCES

Haynes, J. (2004). Behind the closed doors of an ESL classroom. *Essential Teacher, 1*(4), 8–9.

United States Census Bureau. (2004). *Language use.* Retrieved March 15, 2006, from http://www.census.gov/popula tion/www/socdemo/lang use.html

Partnership

HARVEY ALPERT

"The authority of those who teach is often an obstacle to those who want to learn."

—CICERO (106–43 BC)

A teacher must see himself or herself as a partner and collaborator in the learning process. The very nature of teaching sets up the teacher as the authority, the one who always knows the correct answer, while the child is subservient and must please the teacher by doing things the way the teacher prefers. However, it is important for children to learn that there are many ways of solving problems. Hence, when the child is in a problem-solving situation, it is imperative to discuss with children the different strategies that can be employed to solve the problem.

If a teacher simply conveys information and constructs the problem, rather than allowing the child to discover the problem naturally, that teacher is not educating the child. Instead, the teacher is en-couraging children to become dependent upon au-

Teaching With Care: Cultivating Personal Qualities That Make a Difference by Lenore Sandel, Editor. Copyright © 2006 by the International Reading Association.

thority figures to tell them how to do things instead of trying to discover ways of solving life's problems themselves. This dependence is the exact opposite of what we are attempting to achieve. We want children who can recognize a problem, gather information necessary to solve the problem, and then try different strategies without fearing failure, knowing that some techniques will work and that others must be discarded. If we can accomplish this, children will recognize that their teacher is a partner in helping them succeed, not an agent of their failure.

> "We want children who can recognize a problem, gather information necessary to solve the problem, and then try different strategies without fearing failure, knowing that some techniques will work and that others must be discarded."

For example, when children are asked questions and must answer them in front of the class, they are often faced with the pressure of other children waving their hands, begging the teacher to let them respond. This produces stress for the child who is trying to provide the answer because the child becomes fearful that his or her response will be incorrect. When children fear failure, they become unwilling to take risks, which can seriously impede learning. To remove the pressure, a teacher should try reversing roles and become the learner, with the children formulating questions that they want to ask the teacher. In responding to your students' questions, it is important to make occasional errors so that the children understand that everyone is fallible. You also should ask children to find the errors and to tell why they think your response is incorrect. This will empower the students and help make them partners in the learning process.

1st
personal
+
the Instructor

This mindset also should be extended to evaluation. Students should learn that a test tells them whether they have mastered a process or need further learning. Hence, children can be encouraged to mark their own papers and to simply tell the teacher when they feel they have learned enough to demonstrate their competence to the teacher. Instead of grading children throughout the learning process, reserve grades until the final stage of competence. Even at that stage, I recommend encouraging the child to go back and study more to take the test again. Even if it takes longer for some children than others, the children should always be encouraged to succeed. It is the final result that counts, not the process that leads to that result. Again the teacher is a partner in helping the child succeed, not fail.

Trust

& expectations

MARY M. KITAGAWA

"Those who trust us educate us."

—George Eliot (1819–1880)

All students come to school at the beginning of the term hoping for the best year ever. They arrive each day, hoping for the best day ever or, at least, better than the day before. The greatest contribution a teacher can make is to trust students, sharing their hope for a better day by not holding them hostage to events that happened before. If trust is genuine, students absorb it and live up to it over time.

When I reread the declaration above, even I wonder if it is naive. I get a mental image of a teacher standing in front of a class that is behaving as students do in teachers' nightmares and saying in a voice all but lost in the din, "I trust all of you to behave and learn." In my 36 years of teaching, I never stopped having those nightmares at home in my bed, but I found that students do respond to trust, even if only in tiny increments.

When students' supersensitive antennae sense that the teacher expects the worst, they do tend to

Teaching With Care: Cultivating Personal Qualities That Make a Difference
by Lenore Sandel, Editor. Copyright © 2006 by the International Reading Association.

live up to that expectation. The student who knows her reputation for disrupting class has preceded her enters to find herself seated apart from other students or forbidden to sit by a friend on the rug—and the splintered dream of a fresh start drops to the floor at her feet. The same may happen to her classmate who struggles to read, spell, or compute, and finds in the teacher's negativity a self-fulfilling prophecy. These students have been stereotyped and they know it. Sometimes even whole classes carry stereotypes.

> "The greatest contribution a teacher can make is to trust students, sharing their hope for a better day by not holding them hostage to events that happened before. If trust is genuine, students absorb it and live up to it over time."

The old advice to beginning teachers "Don't smile before Thanksgiving" is a symptom of a failure to trust. Escorting students in military fashion and debating whether to be at the head of the line to control speed or at the rear to see all the mischief shows such a lack of trust. Of course, there has to be a compromise among competing needs for hallway decorum, school rules, and the benefits of social interaction between classes, but you can trust students to negotiate that with you. My goal is not to accompany students to lunch unless I need to buy mine or want the chance to socialize with them on the way. If I hear about a stampede, I let them know how disappointed or angry I am because honest emotion is part of trust.

Keeping students occupied with tasks every minute of the day, if the object is only to prevent mischief, is counterproductive. It also creates time-management headaches for the teacher, who has to predict how much time to allow and have stacks of emergency worksheets on hand to keep everyone busy. The workshop model, in which students all engage in the target process like reading or writing, but not in lockstep fashion, takes time to establish but it enables students to manage their own time.

While it is logical to set limits on what can and cannot be free-time activities, whole-class lessons should have flexible parameters that allow students to spend a practicable amount of time and then make choices about how to use any spare time. A good book or magazine, a quiet game or art activity, a conversation that disturbs no one else, a head start on homework, or a long stare out the window are all ways students can be trusted with the balance of time after completing an assignment. In the case of students who have developed a students-versus-teachers culture, nondisruptive use of time will not occur until the culture changes to a trusting community.

I am not opposed to giving such a class age-appropriate incentives to work at self-management. I award "celebration points" earned by the class when they foster a good learning environment; I feel comfortable with the practice as long as the whole class celebrates as a unit and is never penalized for the disruptive behavior of just a few. For several years, I called them "trust points" and used a five-pointed star labeled T-R-U-S-T to chalk in one point up to five times a day in honor of their cooperation. When we had a certain number of trust points, we celebrated with an extra recess.

Trust means always giving a fresh start, whether for the class as a group or for any individual. I have often had students with major behavioral problems that set unique obstacles to the trust relationship I am describing here. However, the harder it is for trust to develop between teacher and student, the more essential it is. It is the fresh start least earned that is most effective. One sixth grader comes to mind: His story resembles those of many angry preadolescents leading to constant disruptions. He shook my beliefs and often made me feel I was being taken as a fool. When I met him a few years later, he told me that what meant the most about being in my class was the way I made it clear that "every day is a new beginning." Through the years, I have forgotten details of most of the frustrating moments with him, but some of the funniest exchanges we shared now stand out in my memory, as I trust they do in his.

As a final note, I do not believe trust has anything to do with taking a laissez-faire approach. It reminds me more of the fence around a precipice at the Grand Canyon. Protected by a solid fence, we can move freely and enjoy the view, but if there is no fence, we stand further back to peek at the spectacle. My students have to know that I am ready to keep them and the learning environment safe, but with that fence in place they can realize their hope of "a better day than ever."

Self-Expression

BERNICE E. CULLINAN

"I fear chiefly lest my expression may not be extravagant enough, may not wander far enough beyond the narrow limit of my daily experience, so as to be adequate to the truth of which I have been convinced. Extravagance! It depends on how you are yarded."

--HENRY DAVID THOREAU (1817–1862)

High-quality self-expression is the ability to say what we think or feel. It is related to reading, listening, and writing—the more we use words, the better we are at using them. Reading, writing, listening, and speaking are necessary requirements for living a full and successful life. A new skill, envisioning, must now be added to the basic skills because we have become a visual society.

If children are unable to voice what they mean, we will never know how they feel. Those who care to speak from the heart display great courage and personal strength. Words carry more than a single meaning, furthermore, words often convey several

Teaching With Care: Cultivating Personal Qualities That Make a Difference by Lenore Sandel, Editor. Copyright © 2006 by the International Reading Association.

layers of meaning. Children who learn to use words carefully are empowered in ways that others cannot comprehend. They can craft words to convey their feelings and they can interpret the words of others to detect subtleties. Both are essential ingredients of success.

> "Children who learn to use words carefully are empowered in ways that others cannot comprehend. They can craft words to convey their feelings and they can interpret the words of others to detect subtleties. Both are essential ingredients of success."

Students who learn to control words can see beyond their literal, factual meaning. They become critical readers who judge the accuracy, authenticity, and veracity of words they read. Reading between the lines as well as reading beyond the lines is a necessary skill in today's world. Children who cannot imagine a world they cannot see are limited; they will never be able to create a better world. By helping students learn to use words well, you will also help them to gain control of their lives.

Many people express themselves through art, music, or dance. I always choose words to express myself because words are the most meaningful to me. I received my greatest joy when I watched a child learn to read and write; it gave my heart a happy charge and often brought tears to my eyes. I taught children in the primary grades for 15 years before I moved on to teaching others how to teach children to read and write. The rewards are primarily emotional and not financial. However, there is no greater reward than being able to help children become all that they can become.

Imagination

KIERAN EGAN

"Imagination...is reason in her most exalted mood."

—WILLIAM WORDSWORTH
(*THE PRELUDE*, 1805/2000, BOOK XIII, LINE 170)

magination is a somewhat dangerous word to add to the list of desirable attributes of any teacher who hopes to be successful in engaging and enlarging the minds of students. It is dangerous in part because of the freight that it carries from the past. Its earliest appearance in the Hebrew tradition comes in the Biblical story of the Tower of Babel. God expressed his anger at humans' attempts to build an escape route from His wrath: "Nothing will be restrained from them, from what they have imagined to do" (Gen., 2:6). The ancient Greeks had a similar story of humanity's attempts to encroach on the power that properly belonged to the gods. Prometheus—"the fore-thinker"—stole the gods' fire and gave it to humanity. One of the subterranean senses of *imagination* is that it represents that part of our minds that threatens the established order of things, and those in power—whether gods, principals, school superintendents, professors, or public opinion—have never welcomed it unequivocally. Calling for imagination, while it may seem innocuous, invites teachers to flirt with something that is perhaps a little more dangerous than a romantic notion of being imaginative might suggest.

> "Teachers who are imaginative not only rethink their own practice to make it vividly engaging but also think about how to stimulate and develop the imaginations of their students."

The modern sense of imagination is powerfully influenced by the way the Romantics used the word to mean the intellectual power that is central to creativity. Analysis of the variety of uses for the word in modern times suggests a core meaning of the ability to think of the possible, not just the actual. Thus, the imaginative person is the one "with the ability to think of lots of possibilities, usually with some richness of detail" (White, 1990, p. 185). That ability to think of lots of possibilities, again, hints at disturbance to the conventional, the normal, the routine, and it involves risk.

Imaginative teachers not only risk the unconventional in teaching but also attend to the imaginations of their students. That is, teachers who are imaginative not only rethink their own practice to make it vividly engaging but also think about how to stimulate and develop the imaginations of their students. To be an imaginative teacher, be sure to focus on the use of those forms of intellectual activity that seem especially able to stimulate imaginative activity. Think not only about the content and concepts you are dealing with but also about the images that can give life and energy to those concepts and that content; draw on vivid metaphors to supplement the logical connections you make; try always to embed concepts and content within a strong and vivid narrative structure; and recognize that all knowledge is the product of someone's hopes, fears, and passions and that to communicate any knowledge meaningfully requires the teacher to show it in the context of the human emotions that gave it birth in the first place.

That last item is important to keep in mind. All the knowledge we have to teach is a product of people's hopes, fears, passions, and other emotions. When we put it into textbooks and organize our lesson plans, we often forget the emotions that were responsible for creating the knowledge in the first place, or attend its use somewhere today. And yet if we hope to engage students' imaginations in learning, it is by introducing the knowledge through those emotions that we will likely be most successful. This does not mean tears and swooning passion in each lesson, but it does mean enlivening each topic with the emotions that make it humanly important. Engaging the imagination is one of the keys to successful teaching and learning, and engaging the imagination requires us to be alert for the emotions hidden in all the topics we teach.

REFERENCES

White, A. (1990). *The language of imagination.* Oxford, England: Blackwell.

Wordsworth, W. (2000). *The major works: Including* The Prelude. Oxford, England: Oxford University Press. (Original work published 1805)

Love

WAYNE B. JENNINGS

"There must be...the generating force of love behind every effort that is to be successful."

—Henry David Thoreau (1817–1862)

ove may seem a strange choice for inclusion in a vocabulary for teachers. It may seem too strong a word for what teachers feel for their students or may carry connotations of romantic love. I mean it, however, in the context of respect—a sort of ultimate liking of every student. Students must feel that their teacher has an unconditional positive regard for them as human beings.

It is not enough for teachers to say they love each student. They must act on it to create an environment in which students know that they are loved and cared for and that their best interests are considered. Even when the teacher cannot abide certain behaviors, the teacher must separate the behavior from the person. An exasperated teacher might say in a difficult situation, "I don't know what I'm going to do about you, Jon, but somehow we're going to find a way to get past this." This gives assurance to the student that the teacher believes in the student in spite of the student's actions. It also more likely leads to a change in behavior. Students want to live up to the expectations of people who like them and who believe in them.

I am reminded of a story about a group of boys classified as having serious behavior problems who were followed into adulthood. A number of the boys had become well-adjusted adults, and it turned out that most of them had the same teacher in common. When that teacher, then very old and in a nursing home, was asked about her methods of teaching, she said, "Well, I guess it was that I just loved those boys."

I speak of love not as an abstract concept. For the human brain to reach its maximum potential, learning must take place in a safe and secure setting. Otherwise, the brain downshifts in some way and excessively filters incoming information for a threat, thereby remaining on anxious alert. This lessens openness to higher order learning.

The teacher who truly loves students makes certain that each feels safe and secure by being aware of interfering factors such as grades, learning styles that do not fit standard educational practices, home conditions, and peer relations. Successful schools and teachers use a variety of approaches to ensure that these factors do not impede learning.

There is little hope of reaching every student if teachers do not like certain types of students. They must love every single one, including those a friend termed "hateable." The teacher who likes or loves only one race or gender or who dislikes "dirty" or "fumbling" students cannot conceal this. At some level of consciousness, students will know. Love means reaching out to all students, making sure every child is treated with courtesy and made to feel welcome and special—even prized.

At a deeper level, teachers must love themselves, for it is hard to feel charitable toward others if you are unable to forgive yourself. The bitter or tormented teacher has little charity to spread to students. This means teacher preparation programs and staff development programs must address the mental health and well-being of teachers. Even the well-balanced teacher needs reminders of the importance of believing in every student. All teachers need strategies to address the enormous range of their students' conditions: out-of-school factors, self-regarding attitudes, peer pressures, academic ability, learning styles, and multiple intelligences. It is not enough to know your subject matter well. Teaching involves three crucial factors: knowledge of the topic, instructional methods, and relationships. Like a three-legged stool, if one of these is missing the stool will not stand.

Love means also that schools must root out practices that demean students. Schools that love children do not use procedures that harm them. Consider the student whose learning style and interests do not match a school's heavy emphasis on classical subject matter mastery. There are many such students who then receive a steady diet of low grades and experience the disappointment of their parents. These students come to dislike school because they believe, probably at an unconscious lev-

> "Teaching involves three crucial factors: knowledge of the topic, instructional methods, and relationships. Like a three-legged stool, if one of these is missing the stool will not stand."

el, that they are disliked at school. We cannot say in such a school that every student is loved. Such practices border on abuse and cause harm to student psyches even when the school is a kindly and relaxed place.

Schools where teachers love students are places of dignity, meaning, and community. Classrooms are characterized by energy, enthusiasm, and learning by all. In such schools, students believe in themselves and grow into responsible citizens, productive workers, lifelong learners, and creative, healthy individuals.

Empathy

KAREN F. OSTERMAN

*"Taught by time, my heart has learned to glow for
other's good, and melt at other's woe."*

—HOMER (*THE ODYSSEY*, 18.269)

mpathy is, or should be, one of the key words in
the teacher's lexicon. An aspect of emotional intelligence, empathy is the ability to be aware of,
to understand, and to appreciate the feelings and
thoughts of others. Metaphorically, empathy is
"seeing the world through another's eyes" or being
able to "put yourself in his shoes." In the classroom,
it is recognizing that the sullen, nonresponsive child
may be deeply upset about a personal matter. It is
sensing that the child who is constantly waving his
hand, calling out with silly comments, or pestering
to help out may be a child who feels rejected and
has a special need to connect with his teacher. Even
while you are struggling to help a student to learn,
empathy is knowing that the child who cannot seem
to pay attention to directions and fiddles during
even your best lesson is suffering because of his in-
ability to learn and live up to your expectations—and

Teaching With Care: Cultivating Personal Qualities That Make a Difference
by Lenore Sandel, Editor. Copyright © 2006 by the International Reading
Association.

his own. Empathy is also rejoicing with the child who makes one small step while most of his peers are racing ahead in the sprint to the college boards, or with the new girl in school who finally finds a friend to work with.

Intuitively, almost all of us understand the importance of being deeply understood and appreciated. We fondly recall the fourth-grade teacher who thought we could be a scientist. We gratefully remember the high school teacher who reached out to us and got us excited about literature even when we were at our adolescent worst. We remember the teachers who saw the best in us, recognized our needs, and excused our occasional or even persistent failures in attention, behavior, or accomplishment.

Our personal experience attests to the importance of teacher empathy and caring; research also affirms these beliefs. The more we know about teaching and learning, the more we realize that the personal connection, the caring response of the teacher, is the bedrock of student learning. When students feel that teachers care about them—in a personal way—they are more likely to be engaged in learning. In contrast, when students have few supportive connections with adults, motivation declines, disengagement increases, and students drop out, mentally and physically. This is true for all children but particularly so for those who experience difficulty in schools. It is the problematic child, the struggling learner, who poses the greatest difficulties for teachers; it is these same children who need empathy most.

John Dewey (1897) tells us that learning is personal and social as well as cognitive and that the best learning occurs when it is rooted in and begins with our personal experience and understanding. Empathy is the means by which we, as teachers, develop a deep understanding of that starting point. Cognitively, what do our students know, and how can we build on those strengths and experiences? Personally and socially, how do they feel when they walk into our classrooms? What is going on in their lives (home and school) that may be supporting or hindering their learning? Whether and how well they learn will be influenced by how well we, as teachers, understand their experience, appreciate and acknowledge their strengths, and accept their needs. Caring teachers show in many different ways that they understand their students—as learners and as individuals with needs, interests, and feelings. They listen, they empathize, and then they go one step further. Because they understand the strengths and weaknesses of their students, they structure a classroom environment that responds to these individual needs. And when teachers recognize and address student needs, students respond with appreciation and cooperation.

> "The more we know about teaching and learning, the more we realize that the personal connection, the caring response of the teacher, is the bedrock of student learning."

In an environment of care, students are more engaged; they also learn more. In the current accountability climate, there is an almost exclusive emphasis on test scores. Empathy plays an important role in achieving even these narrowly defined, but important, outcomes. At the cognitive level, students who feel cared for and respected by the teacher tend to care more about the teacher and about his or her subject interest. They are more interested and more receptive, and they learn more.

Equally important, empathy sets the stage for the students' social development. If students are to engage in healthy and constructive social relationships, they must learn to understand the other person's perspective, and, as research shows, children learn empathy best when adults consistently and meaningfully express the importance of caring for others through their words and actions.

Teachers, then, who take time to see the world through their students' eyes will reap the reward. In a climate of empathy, students are more likely to care about learning and to learn more—not only about science or math or reading, but also about how to establish caring and supportive relationships with adults and peers.

REFERENCE

Dewey, J. (1897). My pedagogic creed. *The School Journal, 54*(3), 77–80.

Caring

NANCY PARKS BERTRAND

"Integrated language arts is more than reading, writing, speaking, listening and thinking. How we feel about ourselves and about others has gigantic impact upon both teachers and learners."

—ORIN COCHRANE, DONNA COCHRANE, SHAREN SCALENA,
& ETHEL BUCHANAN (1984, P. 131)

I often asked my university students, "What do you remember about your favorite teacher?" They overwhelmingly responded, "My favorite teacher made me feel like he or she cared about me as a person, not just a student."

What does it mean, then, to care?

First, care means paying close attention. Second, care means watchful oversight. Third, care means trusting. Fourth, care means attentive assistance or the treatment of those in need. These qualities remind me of all the wonderful teachers I have had the privilege of working with throughout my years as a teacher educator.

It goes without saying that good teachers care about their students. They chose teaching as their profession first and foremost because they care about children. They pay close attention. They know their students as people, not just as students.

Good language arts teachers are watchful. Because they are knowledgeable about content and because they care about their learners, they see how to respond in meaningful and helpful ways. They help their students attach the new to the known, they understand their learners and the materials, and they choose the most appropriate methods.

> "Good language arts teachers are watchful. Because they are knowledgeable about content and because they care about their learners, they see how to respond in meaningful and helpful ways."

Good language arts teachers are risk takers. I believe risk taking is tied to trust. They trust their learners, and so they are less afraid to give their learners responsibility. They allow choice because it is through choice that children learn accountability and become responsible citizens.

Good language arts teachers are attentive to their students and their needs. They know quality children's literature. They read aloud to their classes, regardless of grade level, everyday. They know that students are never too old to be read to. Good language arts teachers also realize that reading and writing are not the only parts of the language arts. They establish classrooms where students engage in active speaking and listening. They know and understand that learning is social and that children need opportunities to share with one another. They understand that learning is often best presented through teaching. Good language arts teachers know and understand how people learn. They know and understand language acquisition and development. They know and understand that people use their language to learn.

Good language arts teachers care about learning—their students' learning and their own. They devote themselves to lifelong learning. They learn everyday from the students in their charge. In addition, good language arts teachers care about content. They are knowledgeable about the reading and writing processes. They are themselves avid readers. They read for pleasure and they let their students know they do. They keep abreast of issues and trends in language arts education. They read professional books and journals. They attend professional meetings even when no external reward is attached because their reward is in the new learning they come away with. Good language arts teachers themselves are also writers. Many keep reflective journals. Some try their hand at fiction; others, at poetry. They write letters to their local newspapers. They demonstrate their passion for reading and writing by letting their students see them read and write. They share their passion for learning with their learners.

When students notice their teachers paying close attention to them, when they see their teachers watching over them, when they believe their teachers trust them, and when they feel that the help they are receiving is in their best interest, they know their teachers care about them as individuals, as people rather than just students.

Good language arts teachers are caring individuals who watch their learners, who respond meaningfully, and who trust themselves and their learners.

REFERENCE

Cochrane, O., Cochrane, D., Scalena, S., & Buchanan, E. (1984). *Reading, writing, and caring*. Winnipeg, MB: Whole Language Consultants.

SECTION III

The Heart of Teaching and Learning

QUESTIONS FOR REFLECTION

1. Consider a situation in your classroom in which the students were not paying attention to the lesson. What difference do you think it would have made to incorporate the suggestions in the essays on performance (J. Dan Marshall), connectivity (John R. McIntyre), inquiry (Beth Berghoff), or spirituality (Susan A. Schiller)?

2. Why do you think essays on serving as a model for students (Rhonda Clements) and encouraging subversion (Lynda Stone) are both included in this section? Think about when it would be appropriate to promote either quality. How might you incorporate both through guidance (Judith A. Sykes)?

3. Listening (David E. Ludlam) and observation (Yetta M. Goodman) are personal skills that take time and patience to develop. Consider how, in developing these skills, you could make your teaching truly adaptive (Lyn Corno).

Performance

J. DAN MARSHALL

"On a good night, I can play the same old songs with new, fresh feelings that I communicate to the others in the band and to the audience. But even on a bad night, when nothing seems to sound or feel right, I— all of us on stage—need to at least deliver the music that the audience paid to hear."

—Anonymous musician

For me, teaching is a lot like performing on stage. (I tend to think of a band, though acting also works.) To make it work, the performer must know herself well. She must play to her strengths and continuously push her limits. No less important, she must know her music as well as her instrument instinctively in order to honestly and fully exploit her connections with them to the fullest. In short, on a good night, a performer relies on routine and convention in order to reach an inner dialogue with herself about her thoughts, feelings, and behaviors as they pertain to the task at hand. From routine comes transcendence and artistry.

Teaching With Care: Cultivating Personal Qualities That Make a Difference by Lenore Sandel, Editor. Copyright © 2006 by the International Reading Association.

Simultaneously, the performer cannot ignore the fact that she is part of an ensemble, which means that her own performance is affected by and dependent upon, to an important extent, those who share her stage. Said differently, she is not only performing for herself in relation to an audience, but no less important, she is performing for and with the others who are there to support and enhance her musical presence as well. It is, after all, their presence that serves to inspire her art.

Finally, a performer can never truly ignore the fact that she is there for a reason: that is, to entertain, move, inform, accept, and transport her audience. If successful, she will enable audience members (with the help of her stage mates) to interpret wonderful, magical meanings in unimaginable ways and toward indescribable ends. So many different listeners with so many different dreams and fantasies, desires and intentions, memories and possibilities—a great performance stirs the lot.

> "A good teacher, like a good performer, must know enough about performing contexts so as to meaningfully connect the performance with life beyond the literal venue—to enable students (as stage mates) to connect themselves with the world *beyond* the moment and with their deeply personal world *of* the moment."

A good teacher, like a good performer, must know enough about performing contexts so as to meaningfully connect the performance with life beyond the literal venue—to enable students (as stage mates) to connect themselves with the world *beyond* the moment and with their deeply personal world *of* the moment. To make this work, you must know your students well enough to permit empathy and insight to flavor your work while simultaneously inviting listeners unlike you to find and define spaces for themselves.

A performer must also creatively and appropriately utilize all of her knowledge and technique. Along with playing skills come song selection, lighting, physical movement, eye contact, careful sound mixing, and, most important, timing. You cannot simply *work* an audience, but you must *work with* your audience, reading their faces and bodies, taking their cues—always willing to consider a change in plans. At the same time, you must—absolutely must—remain in direct, often inferential, contact with your stage mates. You cannot be your best without their immediate and nuanced support, just as a performer cannot succeed without at least the tacit acceptance of her audience. Teachers, as performers, inevitably work both with and *to* their students as audience members.

Finally, a memorable performer must remain true to her feelings, emotions, and deepest beliefs. Those who project honesty and invite their feelings to flavor and infringe upon their knowledge and skills during a performance are most likely to draw equally powerful performances from their stage mates and, as a result, succeed in opening doors for the various needs, desires, and visions of their audience members. Such artists and teachers succeed in connecting honestly with their fellow audience and fellow performers and students as sentient beings, overwhelming the ordinariness of their shared experience by welcoming honest emotion into the moment. Teaching seldom gets more "real" than this.

Connectivity

JOHN R. McINTYRE

*"To be truly educated means going beyond the
isolated facts, it means putting learning in larger
context; and above all, it means discovering the
connectedness of things."*

—ERNEST L. BOYER (1993)

We all routinely encounter ideas we do not understand. When a new or unfamiliar idea con-
fronts us, we intuitively search our memory for
a related concept to create a connection that
will bridge the known from the apparent un-
known. Researchers constantly seek these kinds of
connections in the form of correlations, or cause–
effect relationships, that enhance understanding of
selected variables. One of the functions of research
is making connections among seemingly uncon-
nected ideas. In the process, theory, our best at-
tempt to explain the world around us, evolves.

The term *connectivity* has several connotations in
current educational parlance. Technologically, it is
used to refer to the establishment of contact between

---

points in a telecommunications network. For example, phone companies now provide connectivity through phone jacks, which allows us to use our choice of phone or modem to access the Internet. However, I am referring to a different kind of connectivity: the connections correlated with the development of the connections in the brain. We now know that enriched learning environments provoke increased brain growth and improved mental functioning. Simply stated, "Connectedness refers to the linkage between prior experience and new learning" (Calfee, 1994, p. 5).

The connectivity that teaches estimation can facilitate requires that they recognize and exploit the relationship among concepts and across subject fields. For example, the fifth-grade teacher who teaches estimation in his morning math class might urge in his afternoon social studies session estimation from historical data about the likelihood that Massachusetts would be a flash point for the start of the American Revolution. This kind of connectivity facilitates learning by stressing relationships among concepts. Methods abound to accomplish connections and evoke desirable brain development. Among them are thematic teaching, guiding questions, and cross-disciplinary teaching.

> "Methods abound to accomplish connections and evoke desirable brain development. Among them are thematic teaching, guiding questions, and cross-disciplinary teaching."

Neurological research has found physiological evidence of connectivity using functional magnetic resonance imagery. Thus, we have neurological evidence indicating increased connectivity. Teachers can foster this connectivity and broader understanding among students by emphasizing the natural connections among fields of study. For example, missing numbers in math problems like $5 + \_\_ - 7$ can be related to using context as a clue for word choice, as in *The sleek chestnut pony broke into a swift [gallop].* Pointing out these similarities leads students to realize their connectivity. As proposed in the Carnegie Corporation's report *Higher Education's Challenge: New Teacher Education Models for a New Century* (Grosso de León, 2001), "The effective teacher must develop a set of metaphorical bridges between the teacher's subject knowledge and the implicit understandings brought to the classroom by the learner" (p. 5).

It is these bridges, or connections, that will reinforce our students' mental connections and ensure retention and recall of useful relationships.

REFERENCES

Boyer, E.L. (1993, March). *In search of community.* Speech presented at the annual meeting of the Association for Supervision and Curriculum Development, Washington, DC.

Calfee, R. (May, 1994). *Implications of cognitive psychology for authentic assessment and instruction* (Tech. Rep. No. 69). Washington, DC: National Center for the Study of Writing, U.S. Department of Education. (ERIC Document Reproduction Service No. ED396315)

Grosso de León, A. (2001). *Higher education's challenge: New teacher education models for a new century.* New York: Carnegie Corporation of New York.

Inquiry
BETH BERGHOFF

*"Curiosity, not correctness, propels
the learning process."*

—KATHY G. SHORT, JEROME C. HARSTE, & CAROLYN BURKE
(1996, P. 329)

Children are full of questions, perpetually asking "why?" and "what if?" They wonder about the world they live in, observe it closely, and piece together their own personal theories about how it works. Many times, their understandings are partial, or even wrong. For instance, I remember when my first graders planted seeds in a flower bed near the school, and one student, Brianna, insisted we go outside the very next day to check on their progress. She thought the seeds would grow into plants overnight, like they did in her favorite fairy tale. She was terribly disappointed when she saw the barren patch of dirt and immediately began to ask questions: "Why didn't the seeds grow yet?" "How long will they take?" "Why do we have to wait so long?" Back in the classroom, she began to study

Teaching With Care: Cultivating Personal Qualities That Make a Difference
by Lenore Sandel, Editor. Copyright © 2006 by the International Reading
Association.

seriously the bulletin board where we were charting the progress of several sprouting lima beans. She was full of new questions.

As teachers, we need to assume an inquiry stance so that we are actively wondering about and observing the children we teach. We need to puzzle over the process of their learning. We need to be at their sides as they work and play, listening to their hypotheses and watching their explorations. We need to ask ourselves if we know what we need to know to support them and follow their lead or how to handle it when they present us with new questions and problems to solve. —

(handwritten margin note: Not like meed of what we do)

> "As teachers, we need to assume an inquiry stance so that we are actively wondering about and observing the children we teach."

Inquiry is a stance we take as teachers. Inquiry is also a social process that results in learning. As such, it can provide an underlying structure for curriculum in the classroom. The process begins with time for wandering and wondering. As teachers of inquiry, we invite children to participate in a rich variety of experiences designed to provide stimulating new information and to push the children to the edge of their known worlds. We listen to their questions for our clues about what to do next.

For example, another student, Kayla, wanted to know what happened to a seed after the new plant emerged, so I invited her to fill 20 little cups with dirt and to plant a lima bean in each cup. Once the seeds had sprouted, Kayla and her friends started their observation work. Each day, they pulled one of the plants out of the dirt and drew the seed. This study enabled them to see how the bulk of the seed shrank and decomposed as the plant grew. They also learned a great deal about the roots and stems of the seedlings. Meanwhile, their classmate Lester wanted to know why the leaves turned bright colors in the fall, so he learned about chlorophyll and seasonal weather changes by looking at videos and reading books. Another student, Chelsea, studied diagrams of plant growth and made a list of new and impressive science words like *embryo* and *photosynthesis*.

New knowledge is slippery. Children need time to work with it and make it their own by talking about it, writing about it, drawing about it, or acting it out. They also need the attention of interested others who will respond to their attempts to articulate what they are learning. Given the connections between their questions, Kayla, Lester, and Chelsea made a natural collaborative inquiry work group. They pieced together their bits of information and decided how to share what they were learning with their peers. They created a three-dimensional poster about the growth of plants, which showed plants of graduated heights labeled according to weeks of growth. They were quite content with their work until they presented it to the whole class and another student pointed out that one of their plants was out of order. It was shorter than the preceding plant, and each child offered a different reason for this inconsistency.

Another controversy arose when Lester explained that the plants on their poster were trees, with the tallest plant representing a mature tree. Yet the corresponding label said 12 weeks. When the children were asked if they believed a tree could grow in 12 weeks, they disagreed. One said yes, two said no, and they were off on a new investigation. So is goes with inquiry. There is always something more to think about, always something to add or change, and always a new question. Inquiry is what we know from being with young children. Teaching for inquiry is what we do to support it.

REFERENCE

Short, K.G., Harste, J.C., & Burke, C. (1996). *Creating classrooms for authors and inquirers*. Portsmouth, NH: Heinemann.

New challenge

Spirituality
SUSAN A. SCHILLER

"Spiritual experience cannot be taught. But it can be uncovered, evoked, found, and recovered."

—LINDA LANTIERI (2001, P. 7)

I often assign creative projects when teaching literature to college students, rather than assign an analytic research essay commonly found in college courses. The written instructions set a spiritual tone and tell students to

trust your intuition. Trust your mind. Trust that which you are attracted to and by. Look for ideas and elements in the literature which is repeated or which is connected to themes, characters, settings, literary techniques such as style, structure, and innovations. Look for ways history is used. You might want to respond to the use of prototypes, place, time, dichotomies, etc. You might want to consider cultural messages and devices such as folktales. The choice is yours and the material is rich and varied from which to choose. Be connected to your choice. Care about it. Be thorough. Be creative. Take a risk. Ask me when in doubt.

Teaching With Care: Cultivating Personal Qualities That Make a Difference
by Lenore Sandel, Editor. Copyright © 2006 by the International Reading Association.

Over the years, students have created handmade quilts, oil paintings, watercolors, scrapbooks, original poetry, cookbooks, original song lyrics, CDs, a women's magazine, mini comics, poster art, period clothing, sculptures, culinary dishes, and photo albums. These projects are spiritual, they are meaningful to the individual, they honor multiple ways of knowing our world, and they provide a means by which the students can make the subject matter their own. This exemplifies a spiritual pedagogy and it is holistic.

Spiritual pedagogy is not new. Its roots are traced to the holistic education movement, which began with Rousseau in the 18th century. Rousseau believed that education should seek harmony, rather than simply instilling intellectual knowledge. He was the first to observe child developmental patterns and claimed that children learn at their own natural pace. Subsequent to Rousseau, educational reformists have sought to include the whole person in relationship with the intellectual, physical, emotional, spiritual, aesthetic, and the cosmic or universal context humans live in. For example, 18th-century reformists include Johann Heinrich Pestalozzi, Friedrich Froebel, and William Ellery Channing. Nineteenth-century reformists are Ralph Waldo Emerson, Henry David Thoreau, George Ripley, A. Bronson Alcott, and Francis W. Parker. Twentieth-century educators who advanced holistic thinking include Rudolf Steiner, Maria Montessori, John Dewey, Ron Miller, and John P. Miller. Since 1990, a stronger interest in a spiritual pedagogy has been developing in public education. Educators in the United States, Canada, Great Britain, Australia, and Japan have begun to use the word *spiritual* to describe teaching and learning that comes from the heart and soul. Educational leaders include nationally known teachers and scholars such as Parker Palmer, James Moffett, Linda Lantieri, Rachel Kessler, Nell Noddings, Mary Rose O'Reilly, Richard Graves, John P. Miller, and Regina Foehr. The cumulative work of these scholars has created a groundswell in the area of spirituality in education.

Spiritual experience can be defined in many ways, but it too often carries connotative weight that connects it to religion. This results in misunderstanding and misidentification of what a spiritual pedagogy is or can be. Too many educators mistakenly associate it with religious indoctrination when, in fact, it is actually an approach to learning that is person-centered and highly democratic. To reduce the tendency of connecting a spiritual pedagogy to religion, educators are seeking broader definitions. For example, Linda Lantieri (2001) writes,

> Spiritual experience can be described as the conscious recognition of a connection that goes beyond our own minds or emotions.... [Spiritual approaches are] the kinds of approaches that encourage a commitment to matters of the heart and spirit that are among the positive building blocks of healthy development. (p. 16)

Parker Palmer, renowned American public speaker, teacher educator, and author of *The Courage to Teach*, writes and designs workshops in which he tells us that the spiritual voice is "the voice of soul, that sacred place in every human being where suffering is transformed into creativity and from which generosity can flow" (as cited in

Lantieri, 2001, p. 132). John P. Miller, professor in the Department of Curriculum, Teaching, and Learning at the Ontario Institute for Studies in Education (OISE) at the University of Toronto and head of OISE's Centre for Teacher Development, writes in *The Holistic Curriculum* (1996) that spirituality is the "sense of awe and reverence for life that arises from our relatedness to something both wonderful and mysterious" (p. 2). This is similar to the definition, provided by Ron Miller (1997), editor of *Holistic Education Review*, that spirituality is "some even larger dimension of cosmic purpose, which many people term as the 'spiritual' dimension" (p. 11). My own definition is not so different from these. I believe a spiritual pedagogy begins with but further develops our wonder and awe of the infinite mystery of the cosmos, of all people and gifts of the earth, and of our mental, physical, emotional, and spiritual abilities. From just these few working definitions, we can see that spirituality is easily identifiable outside of religion. Spirituality is a flexible and varied topic that can sustain and enrich education.

While various educators advocating a spiritual approach present differing definitions for spiritual pedagogy, they all suggest that teachers need to enter spiritual pedagogy from a preexisting spiritual foundation of their own and have personal experience with some of the practices before introducing them to students. As in other pedagogical approaches, those who create, plan, and implement workshop activities should aim for boundaries that establish safety for the participants' emotional, physical, and spiritual well-being. Teachers should also provide students with the choice to participate or not when activities may move them too far out of their comfort zone.

What is a spiritual pedagogy and what does it do? First, it is a pedagogy that maintains the mandate to separate church and state, which prohibits public institutions from establishing a religious perspective that all students must adopt. Nell Noddings has a clear discussion of the necessity of this in her book, *The Challenge to Care in Schools* (1992). Second, a spiritual approach develops intuitive knowing and an ability to trust in the inner terrain of knowing and learning. The spiritual dimension relies heavily on contemplation. It requires deep reflection of educational objectivities and activities. Third, a spiritual pedagogy asks that teachers engage in reflective criticism of their personal and professional life experiences, especially about ways those experiences inform their teaching. Finally, a spiritual pedagogy asks for a greater awareness of and sensitivity for all other people.

> "A spiritual approach develops intuitive knowing and an ability to trust in the inner terrain of knowing and learning."

In a spiritual pedagogy, we develop an ability to transcend suffering and to use it to inform our teaching. This causes us to turn to our spirituality and to our emotional intelligence as a resource in professional development (see Daniel Goleman, 1995, for a complete overview of emotional intelligence). Research by Danah Zohar and Ian Marshall (2000) informs us about spiritual intelligence much in the way Goleman has about emotional intelligence. Zohar and Marshall's work leads us to expect the spiritual dimension to evoke spontaneity, acceptance of diversity, and a high degree of compassion. Where does a spiritual pedagogy start? It must start with the teacher's hopes, idealism, and courage to live as a spiritual being. It is essential to open the mind, body, and soul to the transformative power of spirit and to trust that a spiritual approach to learning will guide us to a harmonious and balanced way of being. Spiritual pedagogy is never coercive or forced. As Lantieri (2001) writes, it is "uncovered, evoked, found, and recovered" through experience (p. 7).

Teachers can create and facilitate experiential activities that initiate the spiritual dimension. Such activities might be based in creativity, emotion, silence, visual arts, music and sound, movement such as dance, various forms of meditation, or writing to heal (see Charles Anderson and Miriam McCurdy, 2000, for definitions and practices that bring about emotional healing through writing). There is also a tendency to encourage collaboration as well as a tendency to reject assignments that promote competition among students. When spiritual pedagogy is used, a teacher deliberately initiates the students' fullness of being through classroom interactions and carefully designed assignments. The teacher becomes a colearner, a coach, a guide who relinquishes the role of authoritarian or expert. Pleasure, from creativity and a love of learning, replaces the fear of failure inherent in competition. Friendlier, warmer, supportive relationships grow among students and teacher when collaboration replaces competition. A democratic style of organization often emerges so that each person has an equal voice in determining how learning activities are developed and evaluated. When people share equal power, there is a more relaxed yet animated atmosphere. This makes room for joy, which is contagious. When something feels good, people seek it out. We look for ways to sustain it, to grow from it. The soul, that inner core in all of us, opens to engage with new ideas, new people, new experiences. We strengthen our innate capacity for lifelong learning, and we embark on learning experiences in the spirit of growth and joy.

REFERENCES

Anderson, C.M., & McCurdy, M.M. (Eds.). (2000). *Writing and healing: Toward an informed practice*. Urbana, IL: National Council of Teachers of English.

Goleman, D. (1995). *Emotional intelligence*. New York: Bantam Books.

Lantieri, L. (2001). *Schools with spirit: Nurturing the inner lives of children and teachers*. Boston: Beacon Press.

Miller, J.P. (1996). *The holistic curriculum* (Rev. ed.). Toronto, ON: OISE Press.

Miller, R. (1997). *What are schools for? Holistic education in American education*. Brandon, VT: Holistic Education Press.

Noddings, N. (1992). *The challenge to care in schools*. New York: Teachers College Press.

Zohar, D., & Marshall, I. (2000). *Spiritual intelligence: The ultimate intelligence*. London: Bloomsbury.

Modeling

RHONDA CLEMENTS

"What the child imitates, he begins to understand."

—FRIEDRICH WILHELM AUGUST FROEBEL (1782–1852)

ffective teachers recognize the child's urge to imitate parents' and peers' verbal and physical actions. They make the most of a child's urges by serving as models for the child to copy or duplicate when learning new skills. The importance of imitative behavior (or using an imitative approach to learning) has long been recognized as one way children acquire values, ideals, cultural traditions, language, artistic skills, and even motor and physical skills.

In the country of China, where a great deal of research has been performed on the importance of preserving tradition and imitative learning experiences, imitation is considered the root of preserving the Chinese culture. This belief is based on the idea that young children imitate the actions and play of older children, who have imitated the actions and play of the generation of children preceding them. For example, the manipulative skill of constructing

Teaching With Care: Cultivating Personal Qualities That Make a Difference by Lenore Sandel, Editor. Copyright © 2006 by the International Reading Association.

Chinese lantern frames made of baked bamboo strips bent to the proper shape and covered with cellophane, oil paper, or silk fabric, with a candle for illumination, dates back to the days of Emperor Taitsung of the Tang Dynasty (627–649 AD). The lantern was brought on the first day of school and lit by the teacher to symbolize a bright future. The children painted flowers or applied colorful paper cutouts on the outside. Lanterns are still made today with family members and teachers and come in all shapes, colors, and sizes, resembling such familiar things as lotus flowers and peonies, birds and dragons, rabbits, and goldfish.

To serve as a model and familiarize groups of children with activities tracing back to the early years of the Han Dynasty (219–206 BC), for example, teachers could demonstrate the skills needed to play Chinese hopscotch, Chinese jump-rope, or bamboo instruments. Basic Chinese participatory songs, finger plays, and sand art projects are other group experiences that help to develop social skills and an increased appreciation of a different culture.

From a more contemporary understanding, the word *imitative* has a Latin origin (*imitari*) meaning "likeness." The English adopted the term at the end of the 16th century and used it to describe a behavior that all children and adults exhibit. The use of the term (to emulate) stemmed from the basic premise that humans tend to mirror one another's artistic interests, forms of communication, and even ways of moving.

In the area of music, the teacher can serve as a model and physically prompt the child to follow the words and movements of an action song. He or she can also encourage the children to repeat simple, rhythmic beats using handheld instruments like drums, tambourines, or lumni sticks, or to duplicate the slapping, clapping, and pounding actions common in hand-clapping chants. The teacher might also use music to imitate different types of sounds and moods, asking children to do the same. Like music, dance can be used as a means of expression or communication. The teacher can encourage the child to mimic novel ways of moving, to follow him or her along imaginary pathways, or to reproduce a combination of movements after observing the teacher's performance. In each dance-related experience, teachers should display enthusiasm and great facial expression to spark the child's continued involvement in artistic content.

During storytime or when reading to young children, teachers can challenge children to perform action words in a narrative, assuming the language and body gestures of a storybook character. They can also ask the children to mimic or perform such expressions as "timid as a mouse," "busy as a bee," "light as a feather," "cold as ice," or "scared out of your skin," and use their bodies to convey a wide variety of feelings and expressions (e.g., acting brave, afraid, carefree, fierce, grumpy).

When teaching movement activities, the young child's movement vocabulary is greatly expanded each time the teacher conveys the proper name of a physical skill and then demonstrates the movements for the child to copy. For example, the teacher might say to the child, "Let's pretend to strap on a pair of ice skates. Can you slide and move as if you were skating on slippery ice?" or "Copy me as I make the sounds of a horse's movement, by slapping my hands on my knees and galloping along." or "Follow me while I bounce and catch the ball as we walk."

Successful teachers recognize the importance of learning through observation and demonstration. They realize that many children become easily frustrated and develop anxiety that inhibits further participation unless they have a model to duplicate or copy. This is especially true if a child has no concept of how to perform a task. The teacher should have some discussion of the desired action, followed by a brief demonstration, whereupon the child responds in like manner.

> "Successful teachers...realize that many children become easily frustrated and develop anxiety that inhibits further participation unless they have a model to duplicate or copy."

Imitative experiences do not rob the child of opportunities that would otherwise instill creativity and self-expression. Quite the contrary—all humans need a foundation from which to pull creative thoughts, ideas, and knowledge. The ability to recall what has been observed, and either produce a likeness or reproduce the qualities of the original, is one way the children learn. Hence, teachers who serve as models are displaying a valuable quality for many students.

Subversion

LYNDA STONE

"It is the mark of an educated mind to be able to entertain a thought without accepting it."

—ARISTOTLE (384–322 BC)

I t is the summer of 2005. The United States is at war in Iraq and from time to time there are threats of future conflict with Iran. This is also the year that *Reading Lolita in Tehran: A Memoir in Books* (Nafisi, 2003) is a bestseller. The book is a real-life story of subversion. The author, Azar Nafisi, a college professor of modern English literature, recounts a personal history of the contemporary religious and political revolution in Iran and its effect on daily life. Women are especially affected as they are veiled in a new society. For identity, for autonomy, for survival, they must learn to be subversive. In college courses and ultimately for a secret group meeting in her own home, Nafisi teaches and models subversion.

Nafisi's story of subversion is at once compelling, frightening, and encouraging. It might seem distant from the situations of teaching in a more fortunate place in the West. But as my own students and I discussed, we have our own battles of discrimination and disadvantage to fight. We must, in our daily work, learn to survive and subvert.

"Survive and subvert" is a motto that I tell my teacher education students every year; its corollary is "don't do it alone." I learned this maxim almost 25 years ago when I chanced to meet a remarkable African American professor of English who coined it to share with his own students. I am not sure if I ever asked his permission to pass it on but have remained ever grateful for its lesson and its use. Before turning to subversion itself, a word about survival—while I do think we ought to practice both simultaneously, I understand from my 40 years in education that survival is primary. We must exist, even thrive, within our education institutions each day in order to live for the next day. Some of us are fortunate and our difficulties pale in comparison to others, but all of us have faced adversity. The principal ingredients for survival, it seems to me, are that some of us are hopeful, accepting generosity from and offering generosity to others through our work. Such survival helps make subversion possible.

Subversion is an old word with changing meaning. In modern times, it has not always had a positive connotation, but I believe that it is basically good to be subversive once one understands what the term means. Its derivation is Old French from the 12th century, with appearance in English recorded two centuries later. Initially, it meant demolition of a stronghold; other semantic descriptions attributed

> "'Survive and subvert' is a motto that I tell my teacher education students every year; its corollary is 'don't do it alone.'"

were to turn an object upside down, and even to upset the stomach, in the early 17th century. *Overthrow, demolition, turning over,* and *uprooting* all indicate change—as does the contemporary reference that something that is harmful is in need of being subverted. Subversive action comes from the ground and often may be covert—or initially so. Its need may arise in the immaterial sense of overthrowing a law, rule, condition, or system, or more materially in seeking change in everyday matters. Its effect can be short term, but long-term impact is usually the goal.

It is not easy for anyone to be subversive. However, I believe that educators ought to be subversive. Why is this so? The answer is that hierarchy and, with it, inequity in power relations pervade the institution and the supporting society. This basic inequality—rhetorics of democratic life and schooling reform notwithstanding—is, in my view, fundamentally immoral. The moral educator then is the person who subverts this immoral order, who does not take education for granted, who asks questions, who seeks change, who takes action. One first step toward subversion is to consider the term itself and others like it: language changes practices and practices change language. Overall educational life for many can be vastly improved. Good teachers do their part and they create hope and foster generosity, as they "survive and subvert."

REFERENCE

Nafisi, A. (2003). *Reading Lolita in Tehran: A memoir in books.* New York: Random House.

Guiding

JUDITH A. SYKES

"We are all travelers in a new cognitive epoch."

—ARNOLD SCHEIBEL (1997, P. 23)

One of the best descriptors for teaching is *guiding*. This changes the notion of the factory model of education and teacher as factory manager—desks in rows, lecture-style delivery of what someone has determined is important to memorize and regurgitate. In 21st-century classrooms, teachers guide and facilitate key learning experiences, and research is pointing the way and affirming existing wise ways of teaching based on how the human brain learns best.

To guide learners in their journeys, a teacher must set optimal learning paths, construct the maps for students to operate in, build in reflective processes, and provide the momentum that brings students to new places of knowledge, understanding, and wisdom. It has only been in about the last five years that we have learned almost 95% of what we know about how brains learn. Science is now validating what teachers have known for years—that learning can-

Teaching With Care: Cultivating Personal Qualities That Make a Difference by Lenore Sandel, Editor. Copyright © 2006 by the International Reading Association.

not be a prepackaged, assembly line–delivered commodity. Effective, meaningful learning experiences must be compatible with how the brain functions, guiding students into opportunities to put facts into construction, to work together to solve problems, and to create. Curriculum moves from a need of *covering* to *uncovering* for rich learner connections. With the brain's thirst for patterning and making sense of patterns, learning becomes a student-directed journey guided by teacher rather than teacher-directed lessons.

> "Science is now validating what teachers have known for years—that learning cannot be a prepackaged, assembly line-delivered commodity."

As a student's guide in constructing curriculum knowledge and understanding, the teacher permits pauses on a journey and points out highlights, interesting diversions, and sometimes dangers or risks, allowing the travelers to reflect. Students are supported and encouraged to make their own discoveries along the way. Curriculum becomes a complex and fascinating journey, during which error is a factor in learning. Emotions link to learning and long term memory. Think of the key role literature and the arts play here—how have words and images from authors, poets, playwrights, and artists intertwined with peak emotional experiences most of us cannot easily forget? A humorous story? A stunning work of art? Music that stirs the soul? Materials and activities must have relevancy; we must use multiple teaching and learning strategies as we guide and seize identified windows of opportunity. These windows, no matter the age or stage, are best met using processes of inquiry: questioning, open-ended research assignments, problems to solve, projects to be immersed in.

We are social beings; much of our growth comes from working with and talking with others. During a journey, some will want to travel on and meet the guide later, at certain points. Others will stay with the guide, socializing and clustering among common experiences. A guide cares for his or her followers, forging paths and providing maps to the successful completion of journeys—each at their own pace and style, shedding light in areas of uncertainty. Guiding teachers will watch out for all travelers and ensure that none are left behind. They know each student's journey is his or her own and are eager to encourage, enlighten, and lead along the individual pathways of learning.

More than ever throughout history, students need to be engaged in active, participatory learning and guided through whatever resources or technologies humankind possesses—from ancient manuscripts (some now available on the Internet) to books, software, video, the World Wide Web, and future technologies such as virtual reality. We have connected within and beyond our communities using the earliest technologies such as the horse and buggy to send or receive information or to interact with others; we now operate with global opportunities via chat lines, virtual seminars, the Web, satellite conferences, the media, and so on. Technologies, resources, and networks within and beyond schools, both real and virtual, can dissolve the isolation factor and misunderstandings that are part of the human journey but demand guiding.

Teachers, too, need to be guided by others and work together with other teachers, parents, and administrators in learning about and experiencing their changing role as guide—how this will enable learners to see connections in their learning journeys rather than having them always designed for them. This represents a move from control of people and curriculum to developing questioning and curious people as students are supported, challenged, and trusted on their journeys. Teachers can join or create study groups; become involved in professional associations, listservs, and interactive websites. Practices such as job shadowing, mentoring, and peer coaching allow teachers to experience the role of traveler in the lifelong journey of learning.

REFERENCE

Scheibel, A. (1997). Thinking about thinking. *American School Board Journal, 184*(2), 20–23.

Listening

DAVID E. LUDLAM

"Learning is a result of listening, which in turn leads to even better listening and attentiveness to the other person. In other words, to learn from the child, we must have empathy, and empathy grows as we learn."

—ALICE MILLER (1990, P. 101)

A successful teacher must be a listener. This would appear to be relatively simple to do—after all, we are all listeners. But to what do teachers actually listen? What is it that we hear in a classroom? Obviously, we hear students, but what are they saying and, more important, how is it being said? Given the crowded curriculum and the constrained time frame available for instruction, the typical classroom teacher is often limited to listening to his or her students under what could be considered restricted conditions. Much classroom dialogue is merely structured in such a way that instruction can be implemented and learning assessed: The room is under teacher control, with the students aware of

Teaching With Care: Cultivating Personal Qualities That Make a Difference by Lenore Sandel, Editor. Copyright © 2006 by the International Reading Association.

their expected behavior, raising their hands before speaking, responding to questions from the teacher, and otherwise paying attention to both teacher and classmates. The teacher is listening, but what is he or she really hearing? For that matter, what are the students hearing? Is such a structured process really the way to develop listening skills? Is that what listening is all about? Are academic responses and question-and-answer sessions the only listening procedures with which a teacher should be concerned?

To be a good listener, a teacher needs to hear the wide variety of talk that children produce. If a classroom does not afford the opportunity for true talk—the talk of social interaction, the talk of building social identity, the talk of expressing individual identity—then the teacher is not really listening to the students. Listening is all about talk and talking.

For most students, school is their primary world. It is usually the first place where they are able to experiment with becoming themselves, free from the watchful eyes of their individual families, and on level ground with those around them. The home belongs to the parents, the church or temple is the domain of adult parishioners, the community is structured for adults—but school is for youngsters. In school, children learn to negotiate their relationships with peers and to develop their individual personas. It is through talk that the work of this social interaction is done.

The role of the school system is not only to educate the students in the academic curricula and instruct them in academic skills but also to turn out good citizens, competent workers, and confident individuals. In today's world, the responsibility of helping the student to become a complete person has more often than not fallen to the educational system. If a teacher is to succeed in helping students develop their individual social identities and find their places in the world, it becomes important to create a classroom environment in which students can interact and where student talk is valued.

Both student and teacher need to become listeners. To achieve this, the teacher must allow time for students to talk. Necessarily, that time has to be connected to lessons and instruction, but the structure of the interaction should be natural and take such form that the even the shyest of students will feel comfortable talking.

One means of accomplishing this is through group interaction. Students who work in peer groups, and are allowed to talk freely, can interact while they do various instructional activities, learn social rules, and develop a sense of being part of a social group. Peer interaction activities are essential times for the teacher to be a listener, because in loosely structured situations students really open up and talk without restraint. Listening carefully during such situations, you can come to truly understand your students and to formulate a true picture of how the students are developing and thinking. However, as most successful teachers know, in the classroom, group activity needs to occur under clear guidelines. The trick to accomplishing this is to establish guidelines that are not only flexible but that also lead to completion of the task at hand while facilitating open student-centered and student-directed discussion or conversation.

The teacher who is a good listener lays out the rules of peer-group conduct and sets the task in a clear and understandable minilesson before allowing the students to commence with their activities.

Then the teacher is free to unobtrusively work on his or her own while occasionally moving around the room, listening in on various peer groups and, when necessary, joining a wayward group to reestablish orientation toward the set task. When necessary, the teacher might manipulate the task in such a way as to generate conversation on a topic for which the teacher would like to learn more about the students' various points of view. Be it literature, social studies, or art, students all too often wish to impress the teacher by taking the teacher's point of view or parroting the teacher's opinions. A teacher who is a listener wants to comprehend the true views of the students; only then may the teacher adjust and adapt the classroom lessons in such a manner that they will be accessible to all the students in the room. In addition, understanding an individual student's way of thinking will not only assist the teacher during instruction, but it also will be of benefit in assessing the student's work and subsequently understanding why errors of perception may have occurred.

> "A teacher who is a listener wants to comprehend the true views of the students; only then may the teacher adjust and adapt the classroom lessons in such a manner that they will be accessible to all the students in the room."

As you become a real listener and truly hear your students, you will become more attuned to their needs, point of view, and thought processes and, I hope, become a better teacher.

REFERENCE

Miller, A. (1990). *For your own good: Hidden cruelty in child-rearing and the roots of violence* (3rd ed.). New York: Farrar, Straus and Giroux.

Kidwatching

YETTA M. GOODMAN

"My role...has been to show and prove that children think about writing, and that their thinking demonstrates interest, coherence, value and extraordinary educational potential.... We've got to be capable of listening to them from the very first written babbling—the moment they make their first drawings."

—Emilia Ferreiro (2003, pp. 33–34)

Kidwatching is a concept embedded in the principle that knowledgeable and experienced teachers are always evaluating their students' learning experiences within the ongoing daily curriculum. Kidwatching teachers know a great deal about language and learning and use their knowledge to understand the benefits that come from carefully observing and documenting their students' development in many different contexts because students show different capabilities in different settings (Owocki & Goodman, 2002).

Teaching With Care: Cultivating Personal Qualities That Make a Difference by Lenore Sandel, Editor. Copyright © 2006 by the International Reading Association.

Kidwatchers sometimes step aside from the ongoing curriculum and observe their students writing stories and lists, reading fiction books and nonfiction articles, participating in playground activities, giving and following directions, having disagreements, working at a computer, participating in cultural events, presenting to classmates, and expressing their ideas in the form of drawing, drama, or dance.

Kidwatching teachers listen carefully to gather insight into students' comprehension, confidence, and reading and writing strategies. They discover the experiences learners find exciting or dislike intensely so that they can follow their students' lead to create meaningful and functional learning experiences.

Kidwatching includes formal assessment as teachers interview parents and visit the community to understand the strengths found in their students' cultural and linguistic backgrounds. They analyze miscues to gain insight into students' knowledge of concepts and language conventions. They understand that miscues or errors reflect children's intellectual knowledge, and they use what they learn to develop strategies or minilessons as well as to plan experiences that engage children in a range of language and literacy genres, multiple sign systems, and projects in different content areas.

Teachers document who is using literacy and language with confidence and who needs greater support, who is involved in social experiences and who works or plays independently, which experiences students engage in with enthusiasm and which they resist, and how often students participate in various activities.

Kidwatching involves planned and spontaneous as well as formal and informal observations and interactions with each student. It occurs as teachers interact by asking children to explain their thinking, by conversing with an individual child, and by holding small-group or whole-class discussions.

> "Kidwatchers use a variety of tools to document their observations, including informal conversations, formal interviews, check sheets, observation forms, field notes, portfolios, and home visits."

Kidwatchers use a variety of tools to document their observations, including informal conversations, formal interviews, check sheets, observation forms, field notes, portfolios, and home visits. Observations and interactions often are recorded on sticky notes as teachers write a quick anecdote. Sometimes they tape record an experience for later listening or viewing. Teachers keep track of the date, which kids they are observing, the setting, the content, and who is involved in the experience, such as in the following example.

Notes on Erin (11/19) age 5½ in the library corner: Erin is turning the pages of *Fruits Good to Eat* in order, at a regular pace. She gets to the page with a pineapple on it, looks at it closely, turns to Robin, and asks, "Is this a pineapple?" Robin replies, "I think so, but let's ask Ms. B." They come to me. I ask Erin what she thinks, and she says, "I think so, but what does this say [pointing to the print]?" When I ask her what she thinks, she says, "I think it says *pineapple* because that's in the picture and there's a *p*."

Notes like this are placed in a child's folder and later jog teachers' memories when they expand the notes into reflective statements for permanent record keeping. The notes, tapes, transcripts, and extended reflections are used during conferences with the child to discuss her or his development and to plan together the curricular experiences that expand on the child's strengths. They are also part of conferences with parents and child study groups.

Through kidwatching, great teachers assess their students, involve students in self-assessment, and report to parents. These teachers profile the development of each learner and are able to use the information in positive ways to negotiate and develop a rich and challenging curriculum.

REFERENCES

Ferreiro, E. (2003). *Past and present of the verbs to read and to write*. Toronto, ON: Douglas & McIntyre.

Owocki, G., & Goodman, Y.M. (2002). *Kidwatching: Documenting children's literacy development*. Portsmouth, NH: Heinemann.

Adaptiveness

LYN CORNO

"Being immersed in examples [of student work]...deepens one's sense of pattern and thereby develops the ability to make swift assessments and classifications."

—MINA P. SHAUGHNESSY (1977, P. 5)

A teacher who is adaptive builds teaching activities around what students bring to the learning situation rather than around topics or materials. An adaptive teacher views curricula as fundamentally dynamic, requiring constant reassessment and tuning as instruction proceeds. He or she believes that shifts and adjustments to prepared goals and activities are critical to meeting the needs of particular students. An adaptive teacher actively uses students' comments, observations, work samples, and emotional responses as signals to identify patterns and shape events in the classroom. Adaptive teachers teach directly to the present group of students, rather than to some generic students in the school.

There are a few key principles of adaptive teaching. First, a teacher looks to capitalize on the strengths of the present group of students, while circumventing collective and individual weaknesses. The goal is to enhance aspects of student development over time. Consider, for example, a high school honors English class. When the teacher meets the class, she observes students as *individuals* first. Perhaps her conversations and early observations suggest that the present class group is motivated to do the course work; however, her preliminary assessments strongly suggest that many individual students need to polish basic composition and analysis skills in order to move forward at the rapid pace the course will require.

> "An adaptive teacher actively uses students' comments, observations, work samples, and emotional responses as signals to identify patterns and shape events in the classroom."

As a result, this teacher decides that she cannot start where she did last year. She must teach adaptively. Adaptive teaching might then include, for example, designing some small-group activities and experiences that capitalize on the overall motivation to achieve so evident with the present class, while promoting rapid strengthening of basic skills for the subgroup of students who need it. In this series of small-group activities, the teacher might ask stronger students to support the weaker ones, modeling strategies for interrogating text and drafting. The more advanced students might also be encouraged to assist with dynamic assessments in the small groups as their tutorials proceed, thus allowing the teacher to leverage her own time for the few students who need her most. The teacher effectively brings together a number of well-schooled student aides whom she trains to assist other students needing quick but intensive instruction early on in her course. Teaching adaptively allows the teacher to keep the whole class moving forward in her literature curriculum because the students who assist others during class time are also encouraged to work ahead on their own. The teacher gradually increases the level of work for students building basic skills once they show they can handle it.

Another central principle of adaptive teaching is that, as students gain experience and expertise in the task at hand, the teacher becomes less intrusive and gently encourages students to fly solo. The ultimate goal of adaptive teaching is independent or self-regulated learning. It is to create a core group of students who actively plan, monitor, and evaluate their work as they seek to gain the most from the experience. By increasing the number of students who are up to the work demands of an honors course in this way, the teacher ultimately makes her students more alike than different.

In summary, adaptive teaching starts with strengths and weaknesses the teacher notices about individuals in a particular class. Then, for efficiency, these observations about individuals lead to decisions about how best to teach subgroups of students in a way that benefits the entire class for a certain period or time. As student subject matter expertise increases, ultimately greater numbers of students can work on their own.

A final point is that an ability to teach adaptively is especially important in today's schools. Because student diversity is increasing rapidly, and because special education students now are generally included in regular classrooms, one form of program or curriculum cannot possibly do for all. However, teachers should be wary of directives to individualize instruction; individualizing is over-differentiating. In order to manage the many innovative programs available annually, teachers have to customize and tailor delivery to best suit students in a present classroom. Their charge is not to individualize, but to teach adaptively.

REFERENCE

Shaughnessy, M.P. (1977). *Errors and expectations: A guide for the teacher of basic writing.* New York: Oxford University Press.

SECTION IV

At Day's End

QUESTIONS FOR REFLECTION

1. Many times, sustaining persistence (Hugh Thomas McCracken) in teaching can be overwhelming without support (Michael P. Wolfe). How could you develop relationships in which you not only receive but also lend support to other educators?

2. Take some time to catalog self-knowledge (Gregory A. Smith) of your own personal strengths and weaknesses. Which personal qualities in this volume do you feel comfortable expressing and claiming? Consider what steps you could take to grow into roles that are less comfortable for you. Which qualities would you add to the list?

3. Hope (Ruth D. Farrar) represents more than a teacher's wishes; it is also an ideal for the kind of learning environment great teachers sustain for their students. How might you use the insights in this book to sustain your own hope?

4. Commit to making time for reflection (Thomas R. Hoerr), either in a journal or during time alone or with colleagues. In what ways do you appreciate your own personal qualities and your students? Reflect on your evolving path toward becoming the best educator possible.

Persistence

HUGH THOMAS McCRACKEN

"Nothing in the world can take the place of persistence. Talent will not; nothing is more common than unsuccessful people with talent. Genius will not; unrewarded genius is almost a proverb.... Persistence and determination alone are omnipotent."

—CALVIN COOLIDGE (1872–1933)

If you have sufficient knowledge, compassion, and some humor in your blood, you could almost get along in teaching for a while. You would need one more attribute, however, and it is that oft-maligned behavior: persistence. Persistence is that core that keeps you working toward the sense of mission that motivated you in the first place. Without it, the quality of the experience, especially in the first years of teaching, might be lost.

Beginning teachers are generally assumed to be good if they act orderly and organized, look older dressed, and sound scholarly. As most beginning teachers do not do these things, they and others of-

---

Teaching With Care: Cultivating Personal Qualities That Make a Difference by Lenore Sandel, Editor. Copyright © 2006 by the International Reading Association.

ten believe they should try to get through the first three or four years as rapidly as possible to come upon some steady procedures. However, I would like to make a plea for slowing down by learning persistence while moving easy in harness, as Robert Frost has said, to become an uncommonly successful person with talent.

First, let me say that I mean by persistence a quality of being quite beyond the will to get through something with dogged determination, although that is the base of it. Many people feel that persistence is an attribute that we have before we teach, perhaps a quality with which we are born, and that without it we are doomed to bounce about in jobs and activities, Tigger-like, until we collapse. Hold on. Consider that persistence can be developed and shaped as it faces experiences, rather than preexist as an immutable part of personality. Beginning teachers see a different field from experienced ones. Professional football quarterbacks in their first year are said to see a "slowed-down field" where action occurs indelibly in the mind as all scenes are witnessed without the later discrimination of experience. It is similar for the beginning teacher.

I can recall at the beginning of my own career, over 40 years ago, while teaching a high school sophomore English class, the principal escorting a group of other principals and superintendents through our building in Endicott, New York. He was herding them into a few classes to show off his new batch of hotshot teachers. No notice was given, so when I glanced up from my reading aloud to the

> "Consider that persistence can be developed and shaped as it faces experiences, rather than preexist as an immutable part of personality."

class of about 30 students in rows, I saw a line of suits across the back of the room with a smiling Marty Bortnick, my principal, looking on. I happened to have been reading Dr. Seuss's *Green Eggs and Ham* (1960), and you may remember lines in it such as "Could you, would you, on a train?" (p. 33). Sophomores laughed out loud continuously at what for them were sexual innuendos—a situation which would normally have been mild fun for me, but under these circumstances produced inward terror. I could have been fired for corrupting the youth of Athens, or Endicott. I could have been asked to pause and acknowledge all the school brass. I might have had the students in groups, as I often arranged them, or I might have been reading Emerson or anything that was sexually neutral somehow.

I thought shortly afterward, and I think again now, that it was persistence that saw me through that indelible scene. I can recall physically perspiring, not being conscious of what students were hearing, not even conscious of my own reading, but I knew that I had to finish. I had little experience to draw on: The scene had no discriminatory selection of image in my mind. Later, Marty indicated that his fellow administrators were much impressed. That persistence, almost an externally forced one, helped shape an apparent coolness of mind under pressure. And, as you see, such experiences and the way we learn to approach them are indelible. It happens that I subsequently had many such experiences without getting fired.

I have supervised student teachers for most of my years, and I have seen a number of first-year teachers at work. They all verify by their actions that they once saw a slowed-down field and learned to persist through the bewilderment of excessive impressions. Some would call this development of outward behavior from a quality of inner persistence a show, or performance. Developing persistence enables a habit of focus, a quick assessment of what is important at the moment and what is not. It might appear to be a show, but it is focused attention on the part of the teacher, whom I prefer not to see as a performer but as a scholar. The best use of persistence is to focus on your students, to listen to them, and encourage them to listen to each other.

Most of all, in the process of developing and using persistence, the beginning teacher creates fresh images that are lasting, experiences that shape thinking, stories that instruct, and images whose impact will resurface at crucial times. These images, these stories, need to be valued by sharing them so that others, beginning and experienced teachers and the general public, can see them as valid and useful information about teaching. That persistence that enabled the experiences will imperceptibly evolve into a deeper steadfastness, which will reflect greater peace and sense of purpose to both the teacher and students over time.

Persistence will not only see new teachers through the first years but also will heighten the awareness of that journey and help them develop into teachers who take delight in the sacred relationship of teacher and student.

CHILDREN'S LITERATURE CITED

Seuss, Dr. (1960). *Green eggs and ham*. New York: Random House Books for Young Readers.

Support

MICHAEL P. WOLFE

"Those having torches will pass them on to others."

—PLATO (428–347 BC)

There is little doubt that the initial years of a teaching career are the most important and challenging. Beginning teachers need support from many sources to continue renewing and growing their practice. It is this support that may indeed determine whether a beginning teacher remains in the profession. In fact, some writers have used the Robinson Crusoe metaphor of "sink or swim" to describe the beginning years of teaching. Reasons for early disillusionment among new teachers are numerous and lead to promising practitioners leaving the profession. For teachers who do remain in teaching, it is the beginning five years in which patterns and practices are formed that last an entire career.

The importance of these early years has led school districts to create induction experiences that guide and support new teachers. We want beginners to develop skills and dispositions that propel them along the continuum of practice. Becoming an expert teacher within the first five years of teaching is the goal. National commissions and blue-ribbon committees call for all teachers to be competent, caring, and qualified. This can be achieved through formal and informal support strategies that benefit new teachers.

Most beginning teachers have sobering experiences in the first years of teaching that challenge their sense of self and their own efficacy. Many beginners are assigned the hard-to-staff positions or find themselves in less-than-desirable teaching situations. Beginners assume all the responsibilities of a veteran teacher and may work in schools without a formal induction program. Thus, any support may be incidental.

Teachers today face challenges as never before. The standards movement, high-stakes testing, rapidly changing student demographics, varying parental support, funding uncertainties, and inclusion are just a few of the challenges. Add students who are more ethnically, culturally, and linguistically diverse than anywhere in the world, and a beginning teacher faces complexities that are significant. In fact, teaching has been described as a profession of irreducible complexity. A teacher learns over time within a positive support system how to deal effectively with these complexities. This is more easily achieved and in a shorter time period when support is provided through mentoring, additional professional development opportunities, release time, and an annual growth plan process.

The literature on a new teacher induction is replete with references to poor and inadequate support for the beginner. Problems and concerns identified with new teachers include lack of assistance, isolation, challenging assignments, little or no orientation, exhaustion, and little direction in curriculum and instructional delivery. New teachers have cited a lack of useful feedback and a feeling that they are required to perform as well as a 20-year veteran.

It has been said that these problems confronting new teachers may explain why 30% of new teachers leave the profession within the first two years of experience, another 10% leave after three years, and more than half leave within five to seven years. There is some evidence that the best and brightest are the most likely to leave. With student enrollments climbing again, we cannot afford to lose such teaching talent. The investment is too great for new teachers, the profession, and, most important, the student and society in general.

> "All available education institutions, colleges, universities, teacher centers, school districts, regional inservice centers, and professional organizations should collaborate on delivering beginning teacher induction programs."

All beginning teachers should participate in local programs for continuing education, assistance, and support. All available education institutions, colleges, universities, teacher centers, school districts, regional inservice centers, and professional organizations should collaborate on delivering beginning teacher induction programs.

How new teachers are inducted into the profession will influence not only if one will remain in the profession but also how they impact students. Therefore, I recommend the following core support programs for increasing the effectiveness of new teachers:

- Create time for new teachers to work with trained, experienced mentor teachers.
- Develop ongoing professional development seminars specifically designed for beginning teachers based on needs and current stages of development.
- Provide opportunities for beginning teachers to observe and analyze expert teachers.
- Through a mentoring relationship with a veteran teacher, provide feedback on strengths and weaknesses regarding each new teacher's practices.
- Welcome new teachers in circumstances that foster their professional success and effectiveness.
- Provide new teachers with quality educational materials and teaching assignments that are appropriate to their level of expertise.
- Provide materials and methods to help new teachers have an impact on diverse student groups.
- Enable new teachers to learn to reflect on teaching practices through coaching and training.
- Encourage new teachers to connect with a local university program for continuing their formal education.
- Provide journals permitting new teachers to reflect on their practices.
- Initiate a new-teacher support group.

New-teacher support initiatives vary in terms of funding and formalized structures, but within the variations is the central theme of supporting the continuing professional development of teachers.

Self-Knowledge

GREGORY A. SMITH

"Before fixing what you're looking at, check what you're looking through."

—MARK NEPO (2000, P. 152)

One of the most profound discoveries I made initially as a high school teacher and then as a college professor was that classroom events and relationships with students reveal important personal issues that require attention and resolution. This is an aspect of the teaching profession that no one prepared me for but which has proven to be one of the more valuable aspects of this vocation. Work in classrooms provides an ongoing crucible that demands the refinement of our own spirits. Without this work, teachers at all levels of the educational system run the risk of becoming parodies of themselves, hardened to others and their own best instincts.

Since the range of student personalities and problems is limitless, the people we meet in a classroom inevitably remind us of our own pet peeves and fears. Given the human tendency to reject in others what we dislike in our own makeup, treating

Teaching With Care: Cultivating Personal Qualities That Make a Difference by Lenore Sandel, Editor. Copyright © 2006 by the International Reading Association.

such students with equanimity requires the ability to know the source of our reaction. I regularly encounter students who take on the skeptical and challenging role I occasionally adopted vis-à-vis my own teachers and professors. When this happens, impatience can begin to seep into my calm and reasonable demeanor. Away from class, this student will come to mind more frequently than others; in class, I may even begin to spar intellectually with this young man or woman. When this happens, my relationship with these students remains more positive if I recognize our similarities rather than respond defensively to their questions and attitudes. In time, I come to enjoy their contributions to class conversations and the lively play of ideas and opinions they bring to our interchanges.

> "One of the most profound discoveries I made initially as a high school teacher and then as a college professor was that classroom events and relationships with students reveal important personal issues that require attention and resolution."

On other occasions, some students may remind me of people around whom I felt uncomfortable when I was growing up: the aggressive jock, the kid who tried too hard to be my friend, people who attempted to manipulate me to conform to their will. My tendency was once to remain guarded around these individuals and to erect a barrier of aloofness. The result was generally more aggressiveness, obsequiousness, and manipulation on their part, and more guardedness on my own. I have found over the years that when I am able to see what I am doing and approach such students with openness, we are able to build a relationship upon which learning can be constructed. This does not necessarily mean that the behaviors that worried or annoyed me to begin with disappear; these behaviors just come to play a less significant role in our interactions and conversations.

A similar dynamic occurs in relation to teaching colleagues. I am naturally drawn to individuals who demonstrate a professional presence similar to teachers I have found worthy of respect and admiration, and I am inclined to become distant from those who call up less pleasant memories. Recognizing this dynamic does not mean foregoing the benefits of discernment—some forms of teaching and student–teacher interaction are preferable to others—but this process can lead to a less rigidly judgmental response to people who deserve care and consideration, if not always my approval. If the best teachers are able to make a place for a broad range of students in their classrooms, should they not also try to do this for their peers?

Teachers I admire have the ability to step back from the classroom or faculty room and examine the origins of their specific responses to the occurrences they encounter there. This process requires both mindfulness and the willingness to look dispassionately at aspects of our own history and behavior that are not always easy to accept. Treating our students and colleagues with fairness and compassion demands no less.

REFERENCE

Nepo, M. (2000). *The book of awakening: Having the life you want by being present for the life you have*. Berkeley, CA: Conari Press

Hope

RUTH D. FARRAR

*"I like being human because I am involved with
others in making history out of possibility, not
simply resigned to fatalistic stagnation."*

—PAULO FREIRE (1970/1998, P. 54)

Hephaestus skillfully sculpted Pandora out of pure white marble, Athena breathed life into her and dressed her in elegant garments, Aphrodite gave her exotic jewels and a beautiful smile, and Zeus gave her insatiable curiosity. Zeus also gave Pandora a sealed jar and instructed her never to open it. When her curiosity got the better of her, Pandora opened the jar and released a swarming horde of miseries that mortals had never known before. At the bottom of the jar lay hope. This story of Pandora, derived from Greek mythology, is a great lesson on teaching with hope.

Hope cultivates protest. Often when we look into the faces of our students we see despair—a child wants to give up, and we protest. The signs are everywhere: no homework, no parent conferences, no breakfast, not enough warm or clean clothing, fre-

quent absences, social problems, emo,
and more. We look at hunger, fatigue, ı
pain, and we protest. We see hopelessness,
apathy, or we see hardened resistance. In hop
can accommodate the miseries of our students w
out assimilating them. With the hope of protest w
take on the pain of our students. Because we protest,
we share their hostility, their suffering, and their in-
difference. We raise our voices in protest because
we believe that education will bring new possibilities.

Hope cultivates possibility. Once we have taken
on the pain and hurt of our students, we must transform it. We take their hurt and in return we give the
hope of possibility. We acknowledge students' pain
and we affirm their suffering. The injustice is real—it
is personally real. Possibilities are also real, even
when they are obscured by suffering. Injustice
speaks to the possibilities for justice. As teachers, we
scaffold the hope of possibility. It is possible to find a
book I really like. It is possible to sing in the chorus, to
jump the hurdle, to play the drums, to join the math
club, to have a part in the play, to write an opinion paper for the local newspaper. It is possible; it is critical; it is essential to be a participating member of this
learning community. Hope raises its voice in protest,
and hope reconciles that protest in possibility.

Hope also cultivates power. Carefully nurtured,
the hope of protest and of possibility can produce
the hope of power. Power is learned through the
warp and woof of engagement and reflection. A student learns to learn and finds power in learning. The
hope of power comes not from conformity or submission; it comes when students find their voices.
Voices of power are distinctive and personal voices;

...s of liberation, possibility, and transfor-
...wer is evidenced when people listen,
...licies are changed, when fairness is sanc-
..., when all voices are heard. The hope of pow-
... realized when we step outside the confines of
what has always been—the status
quo—and step inside the demands
for expectation—what should be.

> "...hope of power is realized when we step outside the confines of what has always been—the status quo—and step inside the demands for expectation—what should be."

When our hope is given in protest, in possibility, and in power, our students confront and transform the miseries in their lives. They find power in learning. They use their power to give rise to justice, peace, and transformation in their own lives and the lives of others. Because hope is always at the bottom of the jar, teaching is not a neutral thing. Teaching and learning with hope is a socially transforming act, one child at a time.

REFERENCE

Freire, P. (1998). *Pedagogy of freedom: Ethics, democracy, and civic courage* (P. Clarke, Trans.). New York: Rowman & Littlefield. (Original work published 1970)

Reflection

THOMAS R. HOERR

"In the process of the ongoing education of teachers, the essential moment is that of critical reflection on one's practice."

—PAULO FREIRE (2001, P. 44)

Teaching is an ever-evolving act. The world around us is changing rapidly; you can hardly pick up a newspaper without reading about a technological advance or new insight into how the brain works. Whether teaching younger or older students, leading first graders to read, or helping 18-year-old students grapple with advanced calculus, the superb teacher—the one who makes a difference in the lives of students—is always growing and learning. True growth cannot occur without reflection.

This superb teacher learns from peers, from working collegially with others. Sharing information about students and ideas about curriculum and instruction, learning with and from one another, creates the collegiality that keeps teachers growing and learning.

Teaching With Care: Cultivating Personal Qualities That Make a Difference by Lenore Sandel, Editor. Copyright © 2006 by the International Reading Association.

Professional growth and learning are continual and continuous; they must be! As teachers continue to grow and learn, experience yields deeper levels of understanding. It is important that teachers understand not only how effective they have been, but also what they can do to become even more effective. It is not enough to know whether a student learned; a teacher must understand why and how the student learned.

> "It is important that teachers understand not only how effective they have been, but also what they can do to become even more effective. It is not enough to know whether a student learned; a teacher must understand why and how the student learned."

Reflecting on practice, taking the time to muse on your role and behaviors, and ruminating with others about what worked well and what misfired and why these things happened is essential. Because teaching is an art, not a science, understanding learning and finding better ways to help students learn is an ongoing process that starts with reflection. When it is done best, this reflection is done with colleagues on a regular basis. Whether talking about how the theory of multiple intelligences can be used to help students learn, developing rubrics for use in assessing student presentations, or identifying student work to serve as exemplars, this kind of collegiality and reflection benefits students and teachers. Through collaborative reflection, teachers create and become part of a learning community in which everyone grows and evolves. When it is done best, this reflection is done in a larger context of hypothesis forming and hypothesis testing, with teachers gathering information about what works and what can be done better.